FUCK TRUMP
CATALUNYA LLIURE
I CAN'T
OZZY RULES
PARA LAS MADRES DE LOS DESAPARECIDOS
NOT MY PRESIDENT
IF NOT FOR YOU
PIERDOLIĆ FASZYZM
JUSTIÇA PARA MARIELLE
IMAGINE
FUCK BORIS
PRO CHOICE
PDX!
BOOTS RILEY #OSCARS
43
しゃちほこ

TOM MORELLO

WHATEVER IT TAKES

TOM MORELLO

WHATEVER IT TAKES

GENESIS PUBLICATIONS SINCE 1974

This book is dedicated to all the family, friends, fans, foes and FBI agents that have helped or hindered along the way.

This edition first published in 2020 by Genesis Publications

ISBN: 978-1-905662-63-0

This book first appeared as a limited edition of 2,000 numbered copies, signed by Tom Morello

Genesis Publications Ltd
Genesis House
2 Jenner Road, Guildford
Surrey, England, GU1 3PL

www.genesis-publications.com

CONTENTS

Foreword by Michael Moore

He's not only the most dangerous guitarist in history, he just might be the best guitarist in history. The only truly surprising thing about Tom Morello is that he's still loose!

We now live in a time where he will certainly be among the first to be taken away by the thought police. Fascists, white supremacists, centrists beware: Tom Morello is armed and dangerous, and his weapon is his music.

Foreword by Jann Wenner

In 2009, I produced the Rock and Roll Hall of Fame's 25th anniversary concerts at Madison Square Garden. They included Aretha Franklin, Stevie Wonder, U2, Bruce Springsteen and the E Street Band, Metallica and more. Many guest artists collaborated with the headliners, like Mick Jagger joining U2 for "Gimme Shelter." Tom Morello's guest appearance with Bruce Springsteen on the haunting ballad "The Ghost of Tom Joad" was perhaps the most electrifying. Tom turned the song upside down. He came onstage with his "Arm the Homeless" electric guitar and unleashed a solo that was violent, gorgeous, blissful, and history-making. When you're playing fast high up on the neck, the guitar tends to sound harsh. Tom made it ring and sound like a violin. He also made it sound like a turntable, and blew everyone away when he played a series of octave-shifting, melodic notes, touching the frets from above with his index finger. Bruce, unsurprisingly, asked Tom to join the E Street Band after that for his next world tour.

I learned that performance only scratches the surface of what Tom is about. There's his heartland rock side, which he embraced on the four sensational, underrated albums he made as the Nightwatchman. There's his wild hard rock side, which he showed off in the radical, generation-shaping music he made with Rage Against the Machine. There's also his activist side; he's appeared at rallies around the world for immigrants, nurses, teachers, union workers, and more. When *Rolling Stone* profiled him at home in Los Angeles in 2011 and he happened upon a small group of hospitality workers on a picket line, he had one question: "How can we help?" In every musical persona and performance he is forthrightly, proudly, and passionately political.

Tom graduated from Harvard with honors. It's one of many things he has in common with Barack Obama: Tom was also born to a white Midwestern mother and a black Kenyan father and has roots in Chicago. He could have done anything with his intelligence and drive and he chose to play music and speak up for those who need help the most. He's not only a brilliant musician, but he has a deep heart and a social conscience, just like Bob Dylan, Bruce Springsteen, Bono, or Jackson Browne. Tom is right up there with that gang. I think this excellent book helps explain why.

Foreword by Nora Guthrie

A few years ago, I found an unrecorded lyric of my father, Woody Guthrie, titled "Ease My Revolutionary Mind." Wow! I wondered, who in the world could carry that off with any credibility?

When I go looking for someone who reflects my father's take on the world there's not too many out there that fit the DNA. Because it's not just about singing a protest song. Neither is it about writing a day's reflection on the news. It's not even a commitment to a particular cause to which you lend your name. No. As noble as those acts are, they are *moments* of committing. My father's way was a lifestyle.

He once wrote, "The worst thing that can happen to you is to cut yourself loose from people... and the best thing is to sort of vaccinate yourself right into the big streams and blood of the people." So, this lifestyle thing is about the continuum, the constant flowing into the big streams and blood of humanity. It's an artist who self-describes their entire career this way. It's an artist with the mind and the work spent uninterrupted, with their eye on the prize of a more just world. And when this person enters that path, and finds that trove of justice, they embrace as much of it as their arm span can reach. It's a musician you can count on—no excuses—to always be there. A musician who has no fear, who is not afraid of a good fight, and has no hesitation. So. Who could sing "Revolutionary Mind"? Tom Morello could. And he did.

When Tom Morello sings "This Land Is Your Land" he demands we jump up and sing with our fists raised. He reintroduces "This Land" as Woody's rallying cry to activate the activist in us. I'd never seen it that way before in concert, and I haven't been able to get it out of my mind since.

Items in the Woody Guthrie Center, Tulsa, OK.

Foreword by Chuck D

Tom Morello is a Visionary Activist, meaning what he sees in his mind goes full throttle into him making IT happen. Up to the point of our working brotherhood in Prophets of Rage I thought I was alone in the way I thought about music, culture, and life in general. I found out that my universe lined up succinctly with Tom's and also discovered he had creative galaxies galore well beyond mine...

Fight the Power. Feed the People. Fuck the Gestapo.

HOW TO BE YOUR OWN RECORD COMPANY ⟶

SEND OUT SINGLE OURSELVES

POSTERS, FLATS, PICTURES: SEND TO CLUBS AHEAD (FRIENDS IN TOWN? TO POSTER?

PR FIRM: INQUIRE – GET PRESS

CALL RECORD STORES IN TOWN WE'RE PLAYING – GUEST LIST

CARDS W/ FAN CLUB INFO AND RADIO STATION #S FOR EVERY TOWN

LOCAL SHOWS – INVITE FREE PAPERS TO REVIEW

Introduction by Tom Morello

This is a photo book. A photo book about a lifelong Mission. A mission that more often can be felt rather than articulated. There are clues to the nature of the mission in the guitar riffs, the crazy solos, the lyrics, and in the shared sweat and blood of friends and comrades onstage and off. While this style of illustrative book cannot include every single relevant person or circumstance (that kind of telling may be for another day), it does offer a lifetime of snapshots. Occasionally though, a snapshot bears witness to a turning point, an indelible memory, or a furiously rocking moment on the unpredictable path of that mission. I've tried to collect a few of those to share with you.

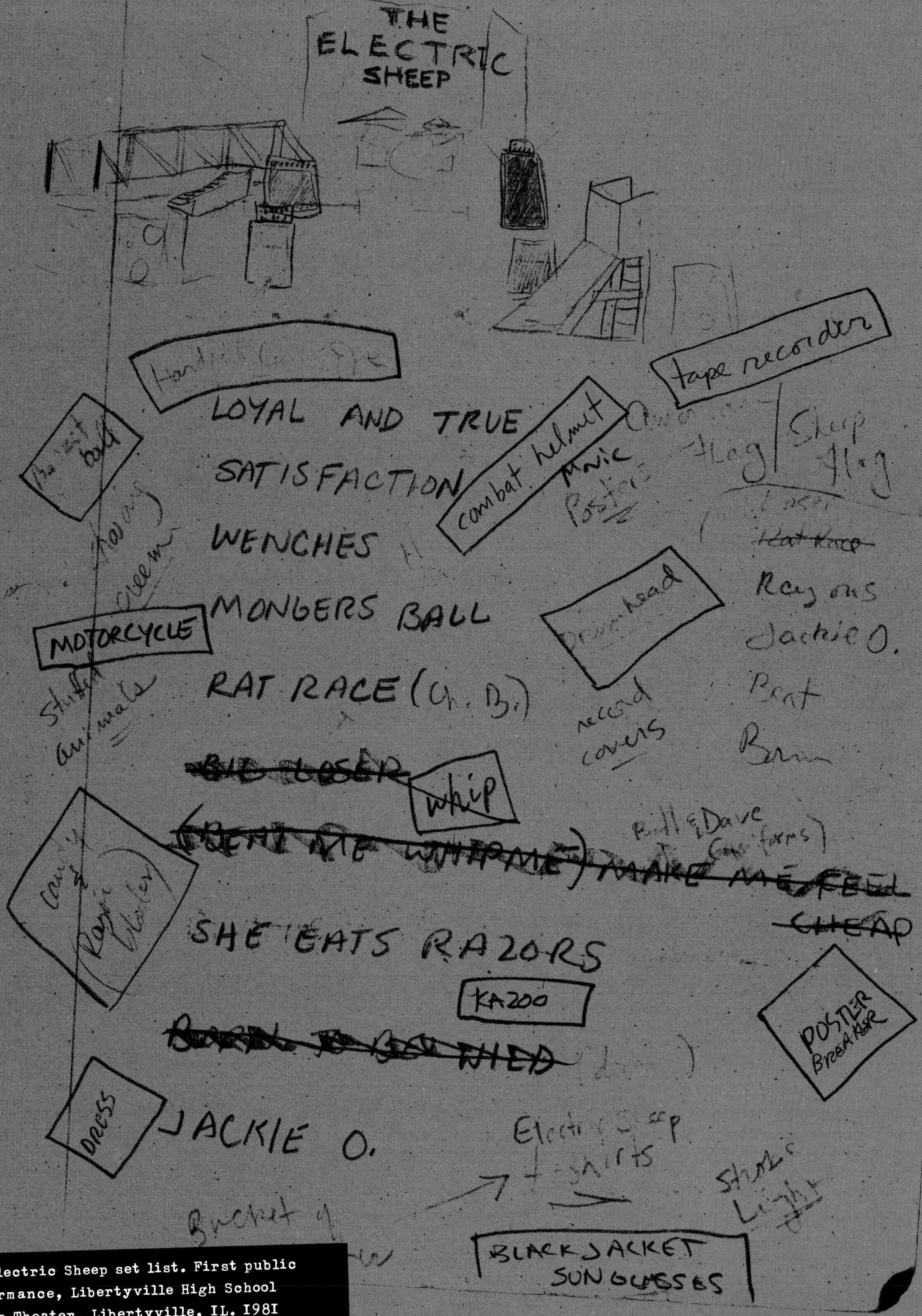
THE ELECTRIC SHEEP
LOYAL AND TRUE
SATISFACTION
WENCHES
MONGERS BALL
RAT RACE (C. B.)
~~BIG LOSER~~
~~(BEAT ME WHIP ME) MAKE ME FEEL CHEAP~~
SHE EATS RAZORS
~~BORN TO BE WILD~~
JACKIE O.
tape recorder
combat helmet
MOTORCYCLE
stuffed animals
Drumhead
record covers
whip
Bill & Dave uniforms
KAZOO
DRESS
POSTER BREAKER
Flag
Sheep flag
~~Rat Race~~
Razors
Jackie O.
Beat
Born
Electric Sheep T-shirts
Strobe Light
BLACK JACKET SUNGLASSES

The Electric Sheep set list. First public performance, Libertyville High School Studio Theater, Libertyville, IL. 1981

Clockwise from top left: Gladys Morello, grandmother; John Baptist “Bab” Morello, grandfather; Isabelle Morello, aunt; Mary Morello, mother; Quentin “Bud” Morello, uncle. Marseilles, IL. Circa 1929

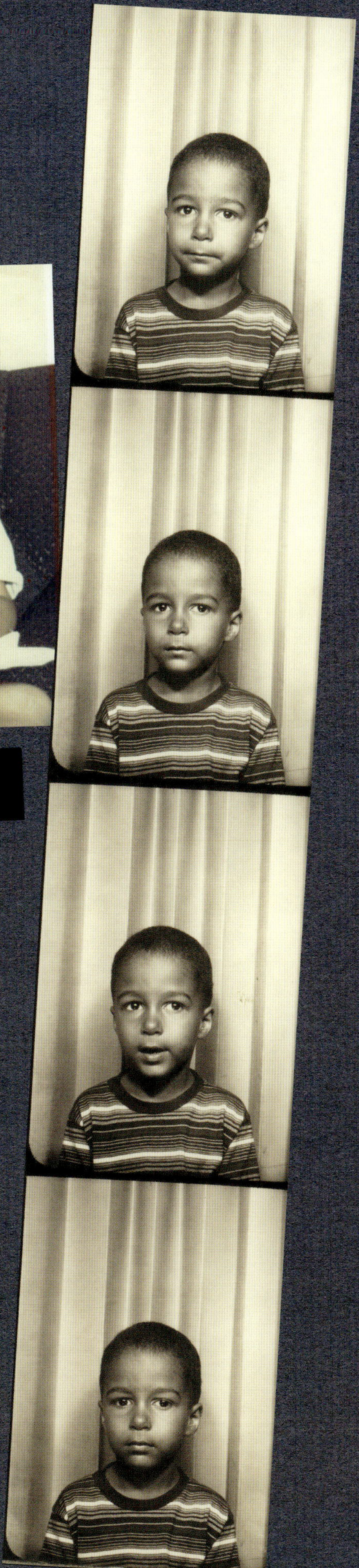

The Early Years

Just returned from my first concert: Kiss at the Chicago Stadium, 1977. I came back feeling as if I had been inhabited by the holy spirit of rock 'n' roll.

On my ticket it said, "A partial view of Kiss." I thought that meant a glimpse into their poetic selves, but it really meant my seat was behind a pole at the side of the stage. It was the most exciting two hours of my life up until that point. I screamed the whole time. Gene Simmons stuck his tongue out at us and we were just euphoric. All I could think was, "Rock 'n' roll is awesome."

My mom and me in our apartment in Harlem on West 142nd and Riverside. The local Catholic church helped my mom as a single mother find a residence, and we lived there for almost a year.

Playing in nursery school in Libertyville, Illinois, with the hair beginning to fly

My father, Ngethe Njoroge, during his eight year stint as Kenya's Ambassador to Great Britain. My parents met in Kenya in 1962.

I was a French horn player at nine years old. I played for a couple of years and after that experience I swore to my mom that music was not for me. Of the four French horn players in the orchestra, I was the fourth chair and I deserved it.

Much of my historic support for the underdog stems from my lifelong love of the Chicago Cubs.

At Wrigley Field with Eddie Vedder

My dear Aunt Isabelle loved the Cubs and lived 82 years without a World Series Championship. When it finally came I celebrated with her.

Throwing out the first ceremonial pitch, Wrigley Field, Chicago, IL. June 20, 2014

My first guitar, which was a $50 Kay, would not stay in tune but it got me started.

My mom and I moved to a house in Libertyville. I would play in the basement with Adam Jones, who became the guitarist of Tool. We did a lot of practicing, we also did a lot of posing. You can see us here, going for broke.

Adam and I recording on my four-track Fostex recorder in my mom's basement

This is my room in Libertyville. You can see my collection of stuffed hippopotamuses. There's a Rush poster over the dresser and a Dumbo piggy bank to complete the look. My stereo is there and my NFL bedspread. You've got to start somewhere.

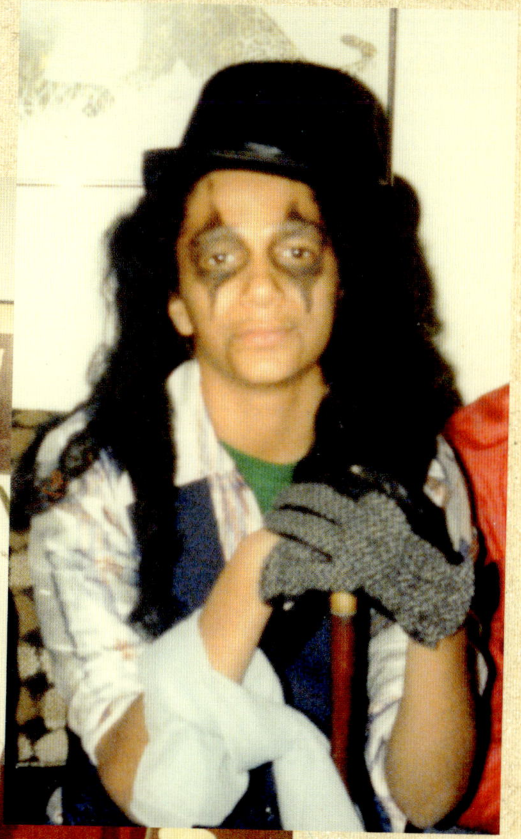

For about six years, every year, I dressed up as Alice Cooper for Halloween. Of the first ten shows I attended in my life, six of them were Alice Cooper. I identified with his outsider-ness, and the theatricality of it as well.

King Richard's Renaissance Faire, Bristol, Wisconsin. I paid my way through college by working five summers at the Renaissance Faire as an actor and musician.

A Midsummer Night's Dream. I played Oberon, King of the Fairies, and I am cradling Puck in my arms.

This is moments before my first ever live performance. It was in my mom's basement with my high school band, The Electric Sheep. This shirt was made out of a garbage bag, held together with red electrical tape. There are exactly 100 safety pins in the pants.

The Electric Sheep flyer with song titles

The Electric Sheep business card. Our manager, "The Shepherd," received one phone inquiry and his parents hung up on the caller.

Delivering a speech at Libertyville High School.

I was very nervous speaking in my own words to an audience. Even in my rock 'n' roll career I was always able to hide behind the guitar. Then later when I was doing my Nightwatchman shows I felt more comfortable opening up, being myself, and telling the stories that I'd been telling my whole life.

THE STUDENT PULSE

ZION

MGA

Naval Base

LHS

LIBERTYVILLE

MUNDELEIN

VERNON TWP.

Ft. Sheridan

US missile base

LET'S SAVE THE WORLD.
STORY–PAGES 6-7

Volume I No. 4 April 8, 1982

One megaton atomic blast

Thermal effects	Circle	Blast effects (excluding additional thermal effects)
Steel surfaces evaporate, concrete surfaces explode, glass windows melt	1	Office-type multi-story reinforced-concrete buildings destroyed
Aluminum siding evaporates, auto sheet metal & lucite windows melt	2	Multi-story monumental-type wall-bearing buildings destroyed
Wood, plastics, heavy fabrics burst into flames; asphalt surfaces melt	3	Unreinforced brick and wood frame buildings destroyed
Upholstery, canvas, clothing burst into flames; painted surfaces explode	4	Unreinforced brick and wood frame buildings damaged beyond repair
Severe 3rd degree burns to people; grass, shrubs ignite; fires spread	5	Unreinforced brick and wood frame buildings damaged but repairable
Severe 2nd degree burns; reflected light blinds people with open eyes		Typical residential buildings usable, but extensive repairs required

Note: Thermal effects are always more severe than blast effects, except for specially-hardened military structures. Thermal plus blast effects will destroy most civilian-type structures.

Radii of circles: #1 — 1.75 miles; #2 — 2.75 miles; #3 — 4.35 miles; #4 — 5.5 miles; #5 — 7.2 miles; #6 — 8.8 miles.

I worked on an underground paper at my high school called *The Student Pulse*, my first foray into activist journalism.

The Electric Sheep, Libertyville High School. 1982

Performing "Born to Be Wild" with The Electric Sheep in the high school auditorium. We were sloppy and out of tune, but when I jumped off that riser the crowd lost their minds.

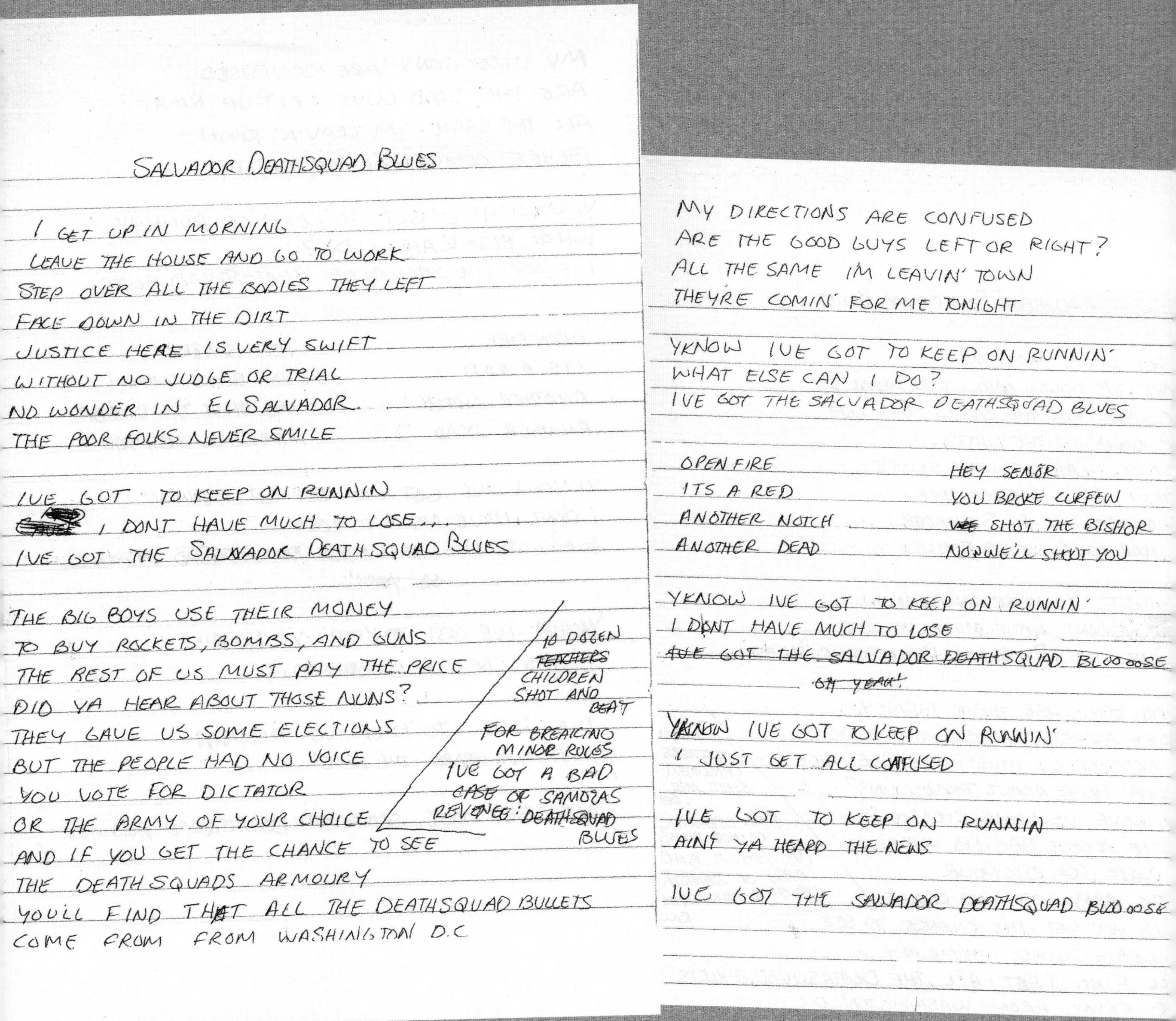

SALVADOR DEATHSQUAD BLUES

I GET UP IN MORNING
LEAVE THE HOUSE AND GO TO WORK
STEP OVER ALL THE BODIES THEY LEFT
FACE DOWN IN THE DIRT
JUSTICE HERE IS VERY SWIFT
WITHOUT NO JUDGE OR TRIAL
NO WONDER IN EL SALVADOR
THE POOR FOLKS NEVER SMILE

IVE GOT TO KEEP ON RUNNIN
~~CAUSE~~ I DONT HAVE MUCH TO LOSE...
IVE GOT THE SALVADOR DEATH SQUAD BLUES

THE BIG BOYS USE THEIR MONEY
TO BUY ROCKETS, BOMBS, AND GUNS
THE REST OF US MUST PAY THE PRICE
DID YA HEAR ABOUT THOSE NUNS?
THEY GAVE US SOME ELECTIONS
BUT THE PEOPLE HAD NO VOICE
YOU VOTE FOR DICTATOR
OR THE ARMY OF YOUR CHOICE
AND IF YOU GET THE CHANCE TO SEE
THE DEATH SQUADS ARMOURY
YOU'LL FIND THAT ALL THE DEATHSQUAD BULLETS
COME FROM FROM WASHINGTON D.C

10 DOZEN
~~TEACHERS~~
CHILDREN
SHOT AND
BEAT
FOR BREAKING
MINOR RULES
IVE GOT A BAD
~~CASE OF SAMOZAS~~
~~REVENGE:~~ DEATHSQUAD
BLUES

MY DIRECTIONS ARE CONFUSED
ARE THE GOOD GUYS LEFT OR RIGHT?
ALL THE SAME IM LEAVIN' TOWN
THEYRE COMIN' FOR ME TONIGHT

YKNOW IVE GOT TO KEEP ON RUNNIN'
WHAT ELSE CAN I DO?
IVE GOT THE SALVADOR DEATHSQUAD BLUES

OPEN FIRE
ITS A RED
ANOTHER NOTCH
ANOTHER DEAD

HEY SENŎR
YOU BROKE CURFEW
~~WE~~ SHOT THE BISHOP
NOW WE'LL SHOOT YOU

YKNOW IVE GOT TO KEEP ON RUNNIN'
I DONT HAVE MUCH TO LOSE
~~IVE GOT THE SALVADOR DEATHSQUAD BLUOOOSE~~
~~OH YEAH!~~

~~YKNOW~~ IVE GOT TO KEEP ON RUNNIN'
I JUST GET ALL CONFUSED

IVE GOT TO KEEP ON RUNNIN
AIN'T YA HEARD THE NEWS

IVE GOT THE SALVADOR DEATHSQUAD BLUOOOSE

Inspired by the Clash's album *London Calling*, I penned my first "political" song, "Salvador Deathsquad Blues."

EGGHEADS AT PLAY

Harvard Bands: Getting to the Hard Core

Would you let these guys play at your bar mitzvah? *From left: THOMAS B. MORELLO '86, JOSEPH M. "JOEY THUNDER" FORBESS '86, GERALD G. ROPER '86, JAMES D. CHRISTIAN '86, and (front) MICHAEL A. COHEN '86 of Joey Thunder and the Electrical Storm.*

Crimson/Jennifer Pitt

I was the first person in Libertyville to ever attend Harvard University; of course, no one had ever applied before.

At Harvard, I formed a band called Joey Thunder and the Electrical Storm. We were Ivy League dudes in full spandex regalia.

We were trying to write songs that sounded like Dokken and Mötley Crüe, as opposed to writing about what I was really interested in. I would try to sneak in one or two songs about apartheid but it just didn't mesh with the spandex.

There was a club in Boston called Celebration that had a Metal Night every Wednesday. We'd go down there because it was the only place you could see heavy metal videos and bands.

Here we are playing an under-attended gig, where our choreography was better than the turnout.

I was pursuing an honors major in political science at Harvard, but the guitar had really become a "calling." I started playing late, at 17, so I had a lot of catching up to do.

I was practicing eight hours a day, every day, without fail in a little rehearsal space near the freshman dorms between the foosball machine and the dryer. In some ways college was intimidating, dating was intimidating, race relations were intimidating. But with my guitar I felt like we were in this together, and with a considerable amount of dedication, we might be unstoppable.

My first gig at Harvard was with a band called the Zoo. We covered Queen songs.

Here, I have my Music Man 4x10 amp in the background. I'm sporting what looks to be a mustache, which is probably driving the audience wild.

The Deviants was my band in sophomore year; the other members were all seniors. It was a working band—we played three-hour covers sets at college parties all over New England and elsewhere. It was the first time I got paid to play rock 'n' roll.

The Deviants had booked a summer club tour in Illinois, and then the three other members quit and everything just went to hell. So I had two weeks to cobble together a band of Libertyville dudes who kind of looked like the original members. We were found out quickly. So, the Gold Rush Lounge ended up being one of our last gigs.

The Deviants

The Deviants playing on the Harvard campus.

Harvard senior year. My band, Bored of Education, won the Ivy League Battle of the Bands.

Prepping for the Ozzy Osbourne Boston Garden show at my Harvard dorm and making the pre-med students nervous.

September 2, 1986. Moments away from embarking on my move from Libertyville to LA in my Chevy Astro van with my co-pilot, Uncle Bud.

I moved to Hollywood with the idea of forming a neo-Marxist funk-Sabbath band. No one was having any of that, so I had to join the only band that would have me, a group called Them Generation.

It proved to be very fruitful because Them Generation were rehearsing in the same complex as my favorite local band, Lock Up. When Lock Up lost their guitar player the proprietor of the rehearsal space, who had heard me shredding up a storm through the wall, suggested they give me a call. So Them Generation built the bridge to Lock Up, which led to my first record deal.

When I joined Lock Up, all the guys in the band were considerably older than I was. I was in my early twenties and I was just doing my best to fit in. We got signed to a major label, Geffen Records. Everyone back home thought I was a millionaire, when really I was eating ramen with six roommates. But it was our grab at the brass ring.

Left to right: Brian Grillo, Chris Beebs, Tom Morello, Vince Ostertag

I would propose *Something Bitchin' This Way Comes* as the worst name of any album ever released. Here it is. Our Geffen Records debut.

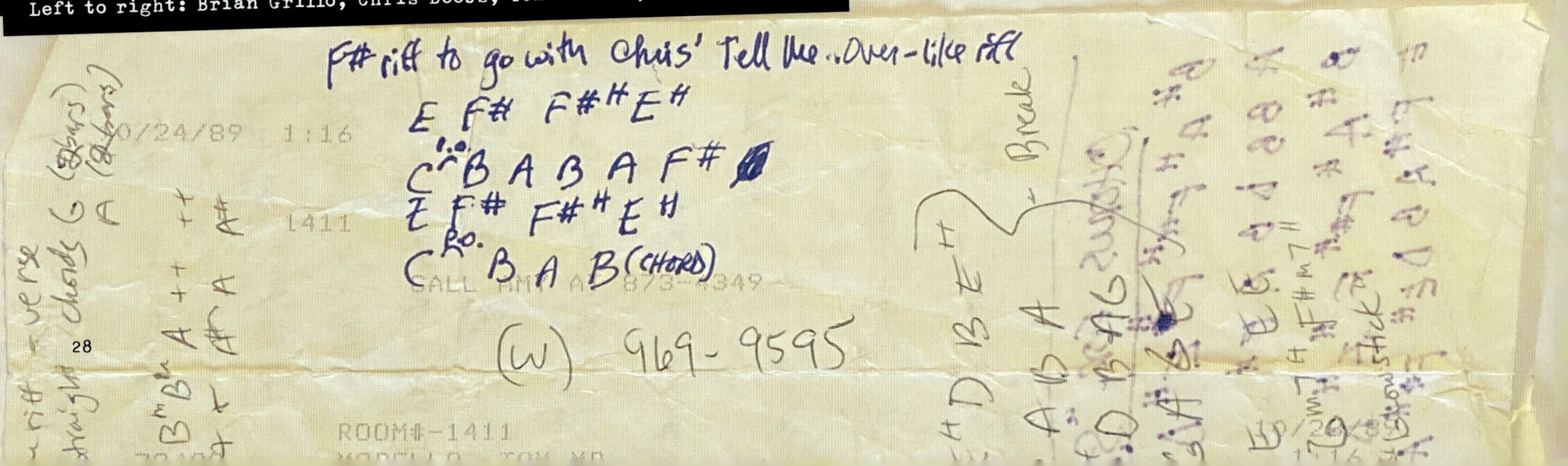

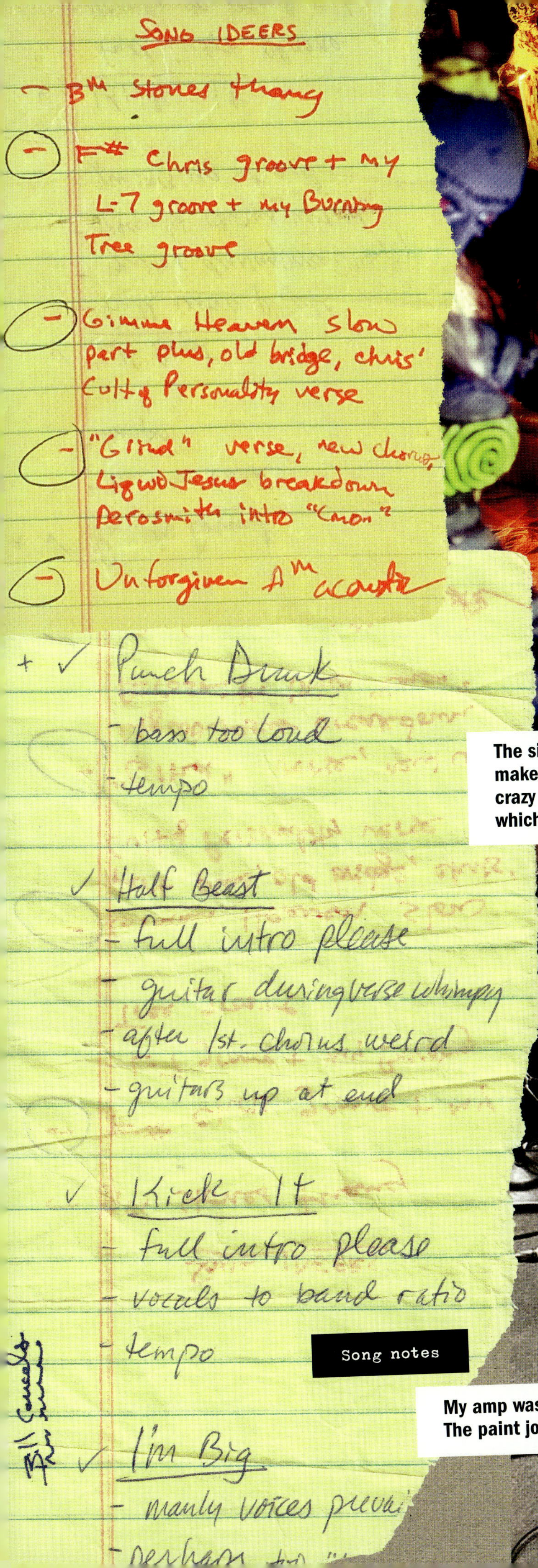
SONG IDEERS

- B^M Stones thang
- F# Chris groove + my L-7 groove + my Burning Tree groove
- Gimme Heaven slow part plus, old bridge, chris' Cult of Personality verse
- "Grind" verse, new chorus, Liquid Jesus breakdown, Aerosmith intro "C'mon"
- Unforgiven A^M acoustic

+ ✓ Punch Drunk
- bass too loud
- tempo

✓ Half Beast
- full intro please
- guitar during verse whimpy
- after 1st. chorus weird
- guitars up at end

✓ Kick It
- full intro please
- vocals to band ratio
- tempo

✓ I'm Big
- manly voices preva

Song notes

Lock Up rehearsal space

The singer, Brian Grillo, was a very talented artist and craftsman. He would make all of our clothes and paint all of our amps. He would make these crazy papier-mâché monsters and glorious neon fever-dream backdrops, which adorned our rehearsal space. His vision was ahead of its time.

My amp was painted by Brian. The paint job remains to this day.

Hippos are literally the only thing I can draw, and I can only draw them facing one way. I drew them on my guitar and then painted them.

Lock Up setlist

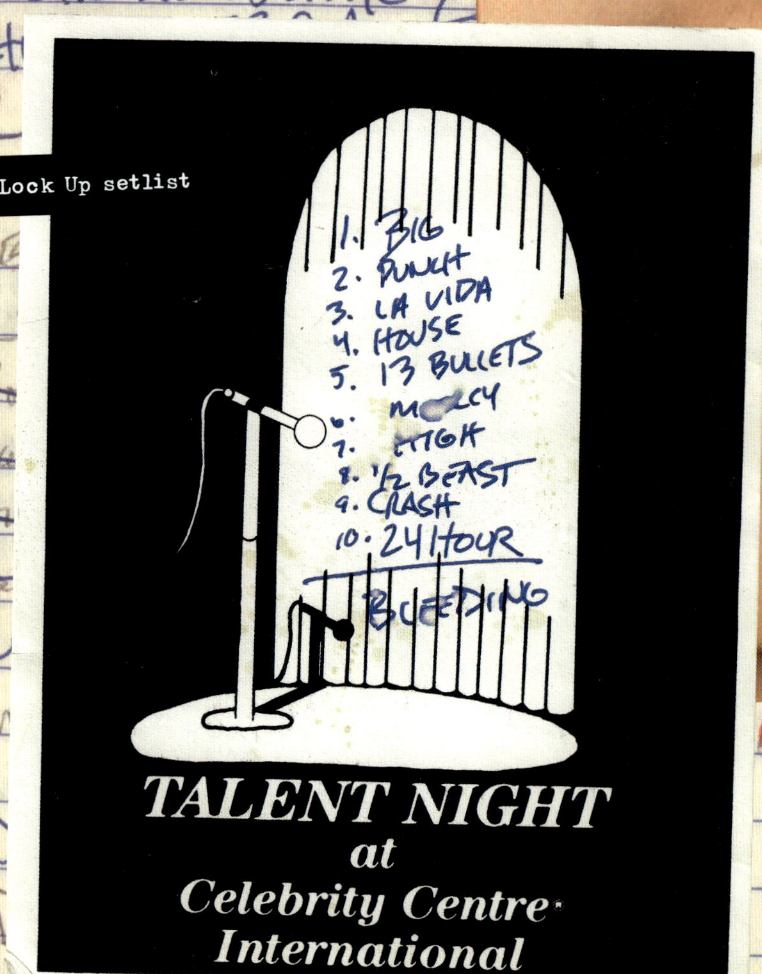

Music Connection

NIGHT LIFE

ROCK

By Eric Niles

Lock-Up

What a week! Missed David

(actually, she's one of the few cool ones), but obliterated it entirely. I won't spoil Laughing Sam's reputation with some generic observation about how they "rilly rocked, dude," but suffice it to say that they were just totally bitchen, to the max and tripendicular.

Also clogging the bill was the delicious retro punk of the **Lovedogs**, not to be confused with the **Lovedolls, Love Razors, Electric Love Hogs, I Love You and Dog D'Amour. Lock-Up** conquered me musical love button as well, especially since they sport a guitarist (**Tom Morrello)** who runs rings around any local axe master around. No more guitar heroes! Theoretically, this whole Whisky she-bang was touted as **The Nymphs'** final show (like the way I get to the meat of the story right away?). Unfortunately, said show lasted a grand total of three songs, at which time, **Inger** punched her own personal Jekyll/Hyde button. Sound screw-ups (the sound was *lousy*) and a variety of other glitches (no candles onstage at the Whisky? Yeccchhhhh!) sent Inger into a tizzy and the boys in the

Jann Browne, Dw... at the Buck Owe...

Mondays at the ... at 9300 W. Jeff... ravaged by a... mental pati... butcher's kn... Gig of th... on the tailw... ing new th... LP, Mar... on July...

...OR SOMETHIN'

F# 3 riffs - Aerosmith one

"Pigs in Zen"

F# F## F# F##

F# F## kick F# A B

Former Soundgarden E riff

G Groove to go with Chris'

C kick E F G Bb G F G

(Pigs in Zen) F slide G F slide G

Groove to go w/ this

F G G# G

** F^G ** Bb^C

F G G# G

** F^G ** Bb

D FUNK SONG w/ end riff from Celebrate

Am acoustic song "Unforgiven"

E song "Grind"

Jazzy song in D w/ Zep like riff

F# minor L7 like song

F# minor Chris's ~~Chorus~~ chorus (vocal twins guitar)

First photo of the "Arm the Homeless" guitar

Raji's was a small underground venue in Hollywood that was later made famous by a picture of Kurt Cobain falling backwards into a drum kit there.

LA Rock Review 5·12·89

Lovedolls & Lock Up

at Raji's

by Ridgeley

Hot, steamy and drained is how most the audience looked after Lock Up finished their set. A non stop hard driving rhythm that had the Raji's crowd rockin'. Lock Up's a band that puts 200% into every performance. Each member being an essential part to the Lock Up sound. Chris and Vince holding together it together with a solid back breaking beat. While Tom wails away on guitar playing anything from power driving riffs and high speed leads, to funk styled melodies. Brian then adds the final touches, being the most energetic singer around. With his strong vocals and amazing stage presence, he gives the crowd a full work out just by watching him.

Lock Up are a breath of fresh air to the L.A. music scene and will soon be displaying their original brand of music to the rest of the world.

Closing the night was the Lovedolls. this might be hard for some people to believe, but this was the first time I've seen the Lovedolls. They blew me away! I wasn't expecting such a tight solid set, and that's what they deliver. Abby, Lovedolls bassist, drills a solid rhythm with the help of drummer Janet. Singer Jenell has a good voice, but it doesn't blend with the Lovedolls music. The Lovedolls will be replacing J... with Fag Hag Lisa Freeman, who will be a great addition to the band. Lisa's vocal's will blend in with music as well as it will with lead guitarist Kim's strong backing vocals.

Catch the Lovedolls next show, they'll be sure to blow your mind!

This was definitely the place to be, even Scott and John were there the dudes with the happenin' hats!

484 0861
Kiva re: 1:30 Easter Egg Hunt
Matt Wallace 939·1765
Cheri re: bowling
Robert re: my missing Dumpster
Bobby — Maynard
Abby re: lunch
Mom re: the party
Kurt re: rental of studio
re: football
re: Too Beautiful for 275 6146

Practicing eight hours a day

We did everything that the record label suggested we should do and then we were summarily dropped. Kicked to the curb with nothing but a couple of hundred bucks a piece and shattered dreams to show for our time at Geffen. I was 27 years old and I had failed in my quest to become a rock star.

But I was still a musician. On that day I vowed that I would never play another note of music that I didn't believe in and started fiddling around with some riffs that would eventually form my contributions to the first Rage Against the Machine record.

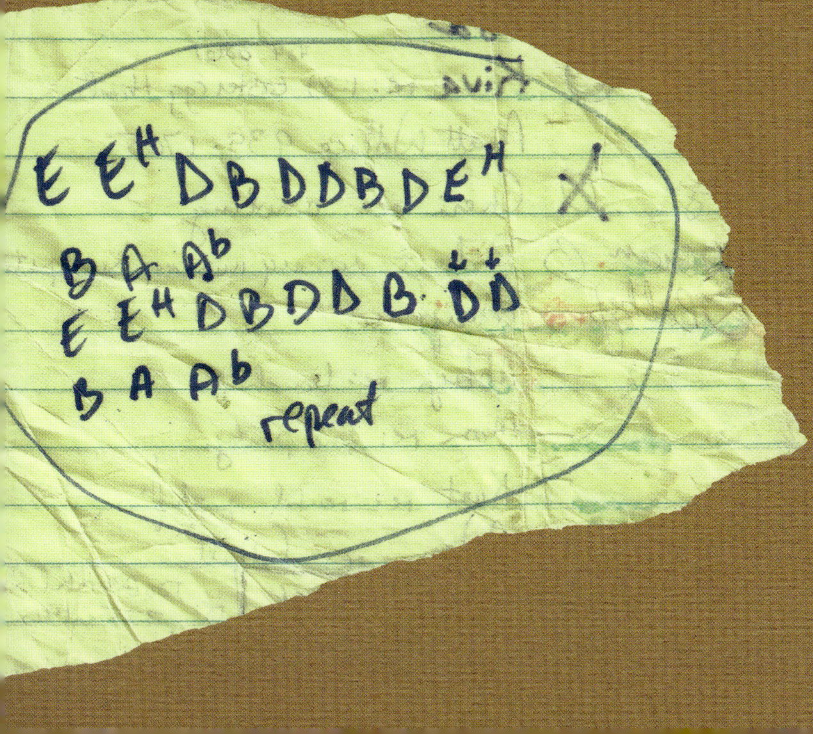

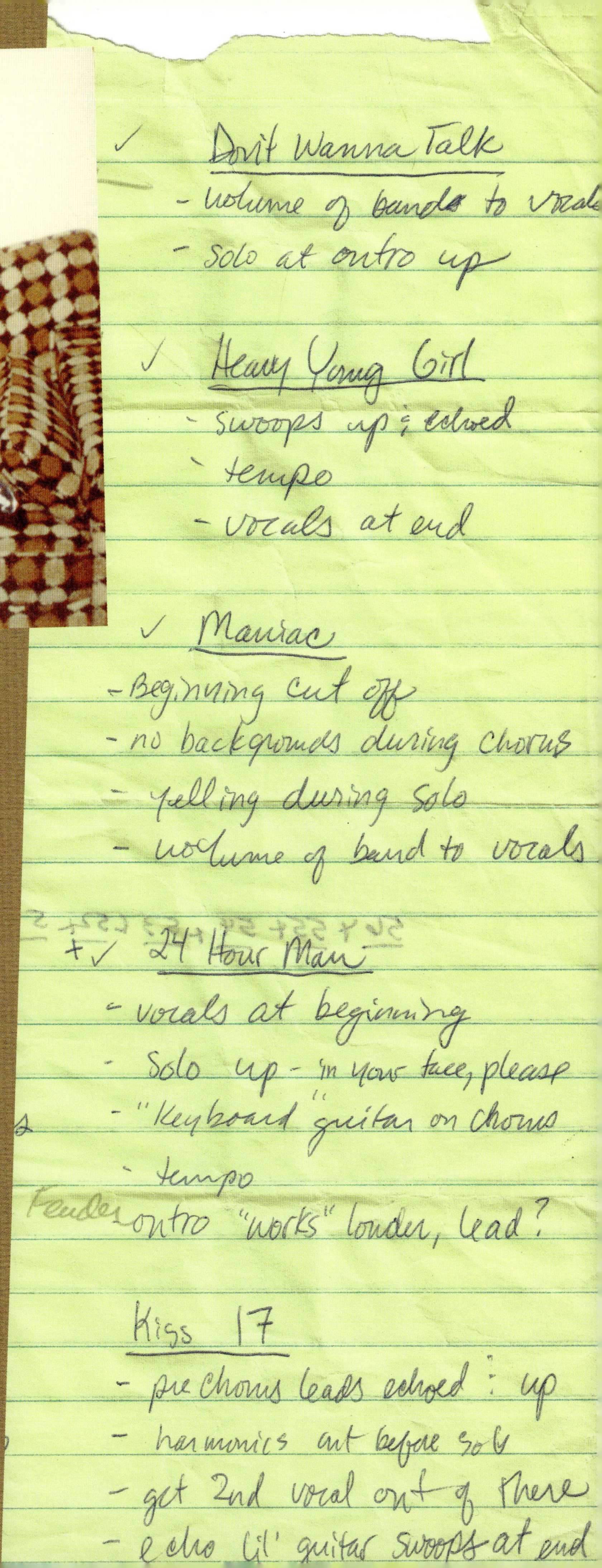

THE BATTLE OF
FINSBURY PARK
JUNE 6, 2010

- TESTIFY
- BOMBTRACK
- PEOPLE OF THE SUN
- KNOW YOUR ENEMY
- BULLS ON PARADE
- TOWNSHIP REBELLION
- BULLET IN THE HEAD
- WHITE RIOT
- GUERRILLA RADIO
- SLEEP NOW
- FREEDOM

- KILLING IN THE NAME

Rage Against The Machine

Castaic Lake, near Los Angeles. July II, 1992

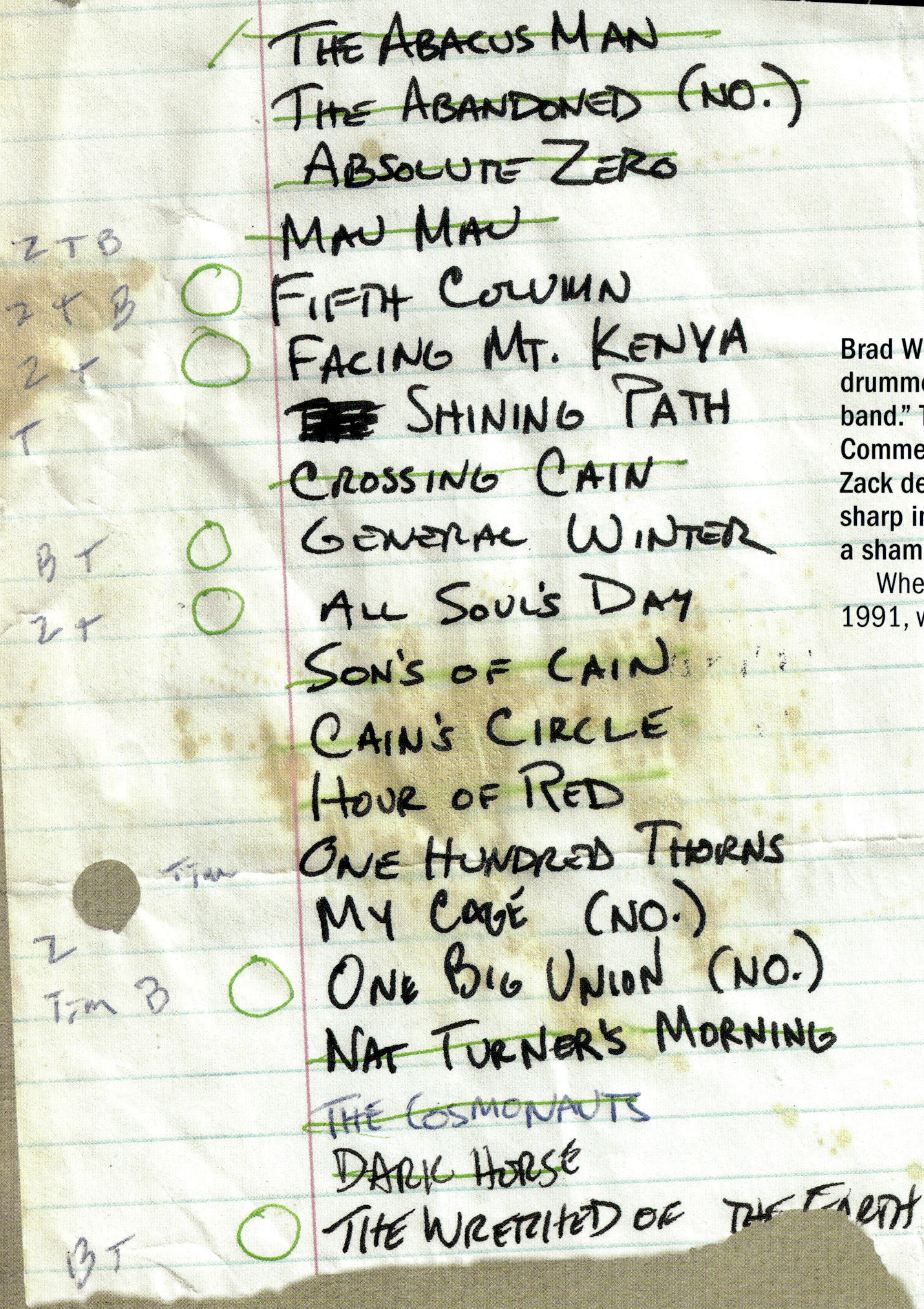

Rejected band names

Brad Wilk put an ad in the paper that said, "Hard-hitting drummer, plays like John Bonham meets James Brown, seeks band." That was a very accurate description of his playing. Tim Commerford was a monster bass player with a ferocious tone. Zack de la Rocha was a punk rock James Brown with razor sharp insightful lyrics, hardcore political commitment, and a shaman-like fury on stage.

When the four of us first played together at the end of August 1991, we already sounded like Rage Against the Machine.

California State University, Northridge. October 23, 1991

I didn't think we'd even be able to book a club show because there were no bands that looked like us, sounded like us, or had our uncompromising political intent playing locally, let alone making records. We wrote 14 songs, never really expecting anyone else to hear them. Those songs formed most of the first Rage Against the Machine record.

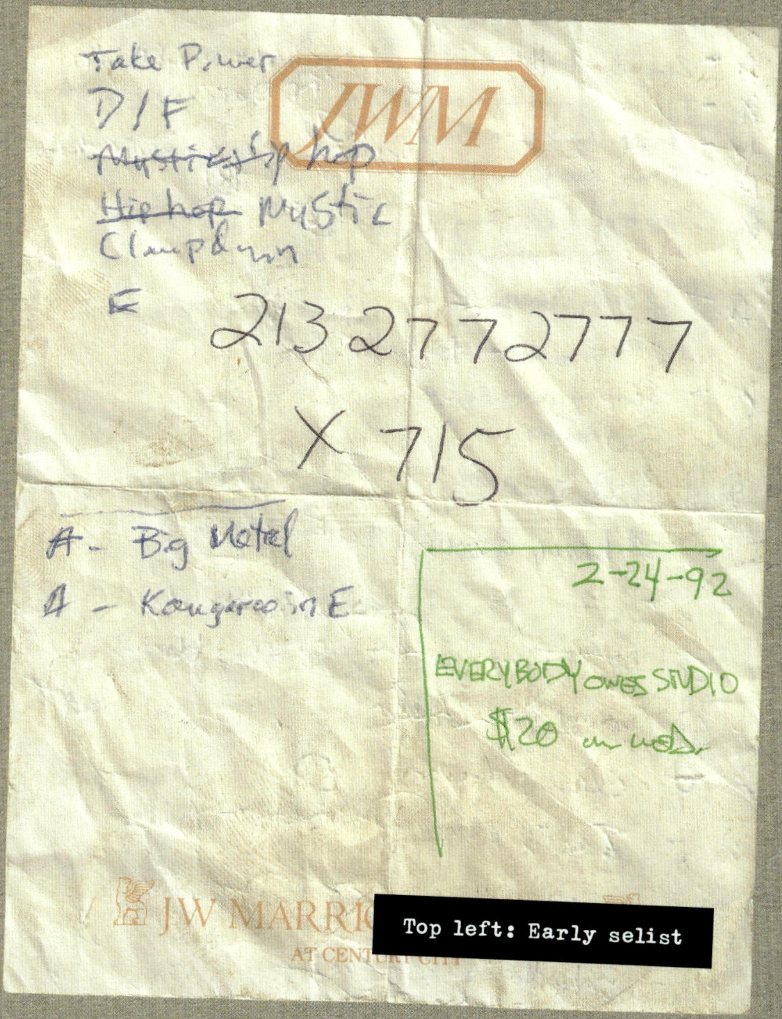

Top left: Early selist

Our first public performance was a Cal State Northridge lunchtime concert. We opened with an instrumental arrangement of "Killing in the Name." I've seen the video of this show online and it sounds like Rage Against the Machine right off the bat. It's like we came out of the womb fully formed.

People were walking by with their lunch trays, but then a couple of metal dudes stopped when they heard the end of "Bullet in the Head" and started to bang their heads. By the end, there was a guy doing a crazy hippie dance at the front of the stage and we were definitely on our way.

From our earliest club gigs, the audience lost their fucking minds.

The idea of a record deal wasn't in our universe. We had no commercial ambitions whatsoever. But bands like Nirvana and Pearl Jam were ascendant and record companies had to contend with a new kind of artist.

Club Lingerie, Los Angeles. December 12, 1991

Club Lingerie, Los Angeles. January 23, 1992

Tool at the Jellö Loft, Los Angeles. December 31, 1991

When Tool signed a record deal, they threw a party. Rage and Tool both played with about 12 people in the audience.

We were good friends with the guys in Tool. I'd known Adam forever, and the singer, Maynard Keenan, had been my roommate for a while. We played a lot of shows early on and really pushed each other.

Wetlands, New York City. January 20, 1993

The first Rage Against the Machine album was recorded at Sound City in Van Nuys, California. Garth "GGGarth" Richardson was the producer. After failed experiments of renting new, shiny gear, we went back to what we knew best. We invited a bunch of friends to the studio, rocked the set a couple times through, and that night captured six takes that eventually appeared on the debut album.

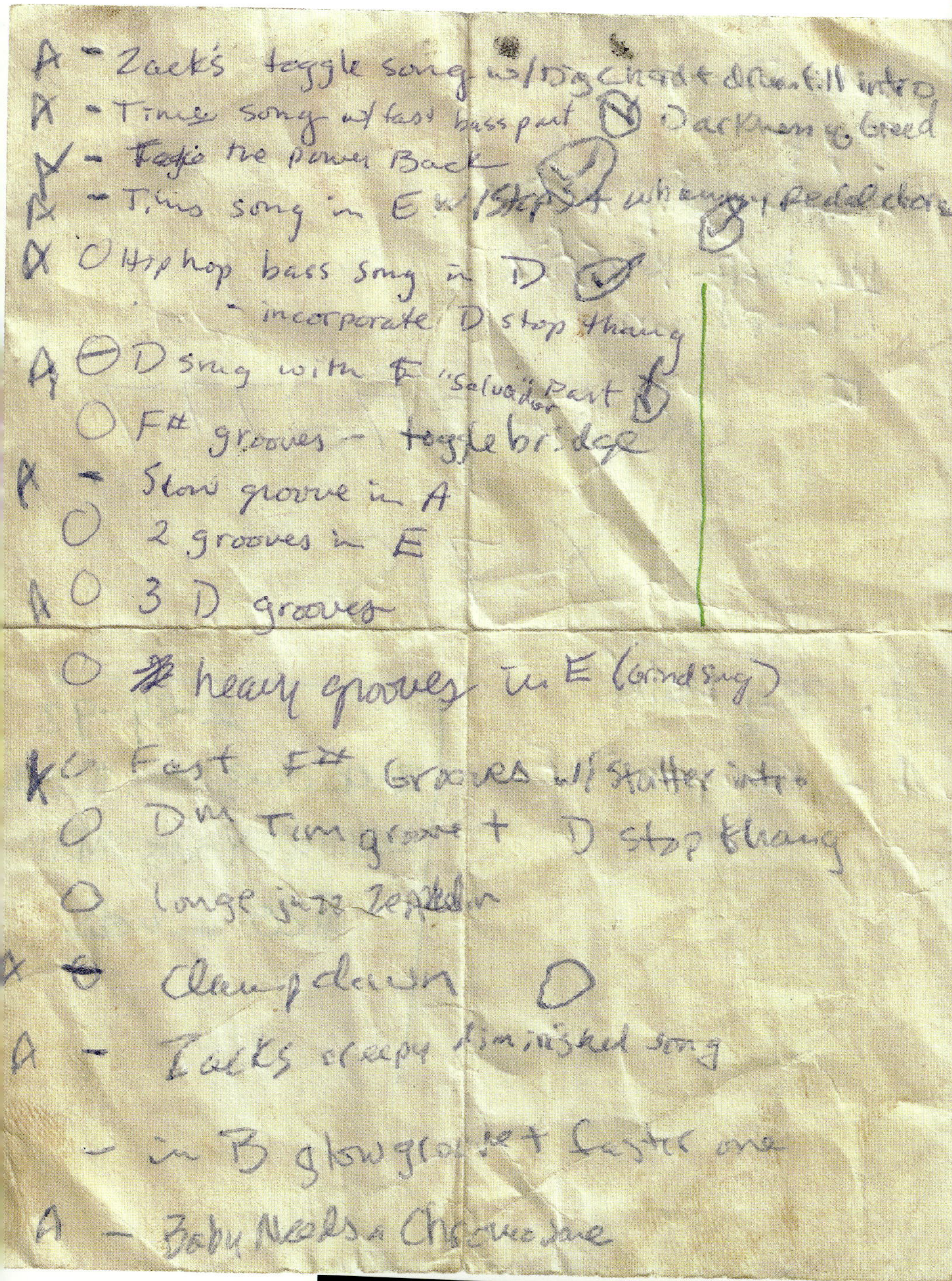

A - Zack's toggle song w/ big chord + drum fill intro
A - Tim's song w/ fast bass part Darkness of Greed
A - Take the Power Back
A - Tim's song in E w/ stop + whammy pedal chorus
A Hip hop bass song in D
- incorporate D stop thang
A D song with E "Salvador" part
F# grooves - toggle bridge
A - Slow groove in A
2 grooves in E
A 3 D grooves
heavy grooves in E (Grind song)
A Fast F# Grooves w/ stutter intro
Dm Tim groove + D stop thang
lounge jazz Zeppelin
A Clampdown
A - Zacks creepy diminished song
- in B slow groove + faster one
A - Baby Needs a Chromosome

Working song titles from early Rage rehearsals

Sound City Studios. 1992

Palace, Los Angeles. February 4, 1992

For our tenth show, we opened up for Body Count. The photograph on the back of the debut album was taken that night (below).

We did a West Coast swing with Public Enemy in 1992, our first "tour." It was an honor to share the stage with our heroes.

New York City, NY. March, 1993

Castaic Lake, near Los Angeles. July II, 1992

Hollywood Palladium, Los Angeles. May 13, 1992

When we opened up for Pearl Jam at the Hollywood Palladium, we passed out our demo tape at the end of the show. The cassette cover features stock market prices with a real match taped to each one. As we were handing out the tapes it was like a piranha frenzy.

There was an early show where Tom Araya, the singer of Slayer, waited in line and gave me his $5 for our tape without any fanfare. I thought, "He understands."

Castaic Lake, near Los Angeles. July II, 1992

Opening for Porno for Pyros, which was Perry Farrell and Stephen Perkins's post-Jane's Addiction band. It was a big jump in size of venue. There were 5,000 people at Castaic Lake and we murdered it.

Club with No Name, Los Angeles. August 3, 1992

The video for "Killing in the Name" was shot here by Peter Gideon, a local musician who was a guitar student of mine. The total cost for that video was around $500.

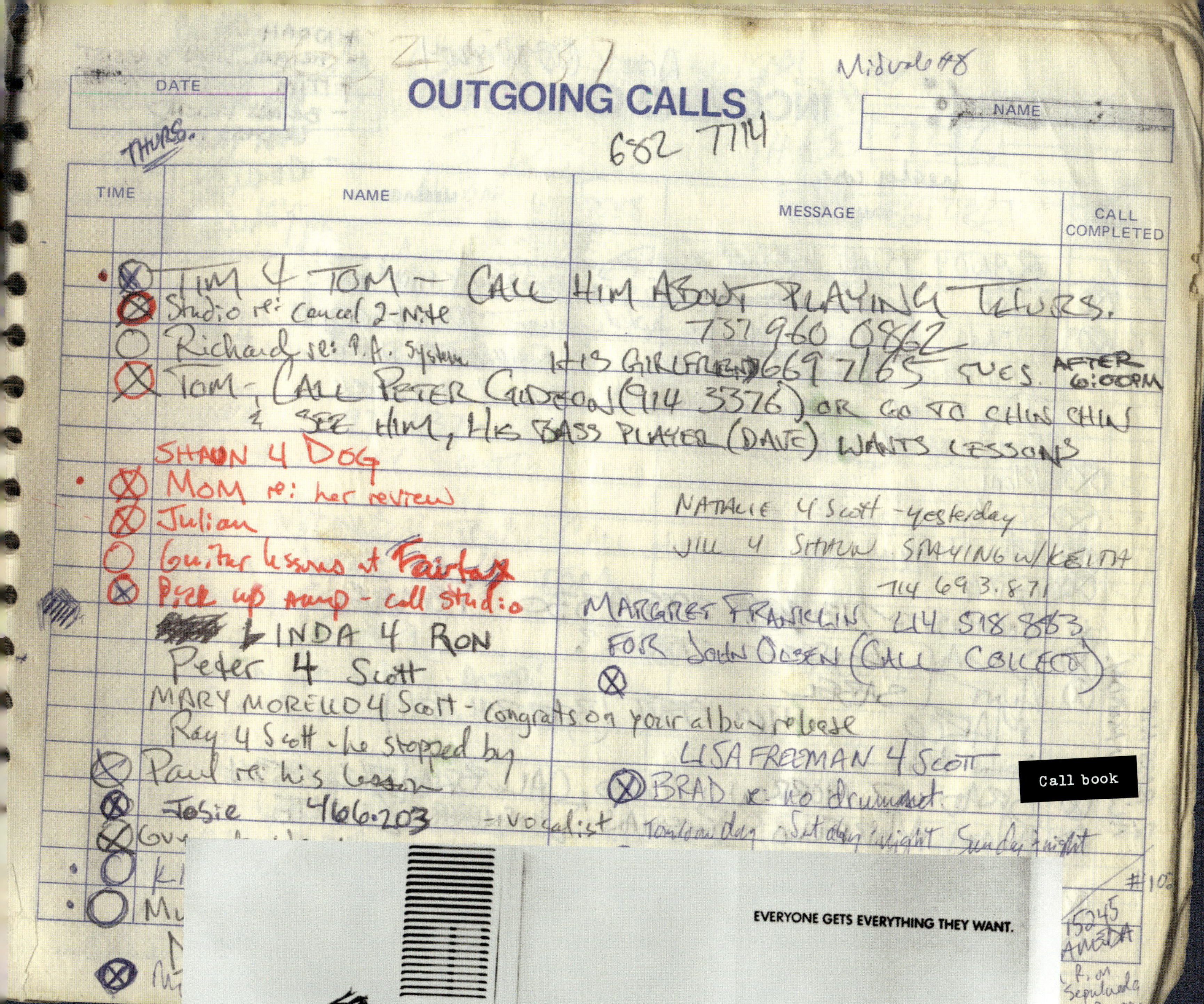

DATE
THURS.

OUTGOING CALLS

682 7714

Midvale 48

NAME

TIME		NAME	MESSAGE	CALL COMPLETED
⊗		TIM 4 TOM – CALL HIM ABOUT PLAYING THURS.		
⊗		Studio re: Cancel 2-Nite	737 960 0862	
○		Richard re: P.A. System	HIS GIRLFRIEND 669 7165 TUES.	AFTER 6:00PM
⊗		TOM – CALL PETER GIDEON (914 3376) OR GO TO CHIN CHIN & SEE HIM, HIS BASS PLAYER (DAVE) WANTS LESSONS		
		SHAWN 4 DOG		
⊗		MOM re: her review	NATALIE 4 Scott – yesterday	
⊗		Julian	JILL 4 SHAWN STAYING w/ KEITH	
○		Guitar lessons at Fairfax	714 693.871	
⊗		Pick up amp – call studio	MARGRET FRANKLIN 714 518 8863	
		LINDA 4 RON	FOR JOHN OLSEN (CALL COLLECT)	
		Peter 4 Scott	⊗	
		MARY MORELLO 4 Scott – Congrats on your album release		
		Ray 4 Scott – he stopped by	LISA FREEMAN 4 SCOTT	
⊗		Paul re: his lesson	⊗ BRAD re: no drummer	
⊗		Josie 466.203 – vocalist	Tomorrow day – Saturday night – Sunday night	

#102
15245
AMEDA

Call book

Hancock Avenue, Los Angeles. June 3, 1992

Despite our high-profile opening slots, we couldn't get any traction in the US. But in the UK it was a different story. We played numerous TV and radio shows and then we had a "Sex Pistols moment" when a major BBC radio station played "Killing in the Name" uncensored. In the aftermath, we became pop stars. There were kids sleeping in the lobbies of our hotels and following us in crowds down the street.

It was weird, because back home we were opening up for House of Pain in half-empty clubs.

Hancock Avenue, Los Angeles. June 3, 1992

Taken in the laundry room of my apartment complex

Originally, the "Arm the Homeless" guitar was custom made in a small shop in Hollywood. It was virtually unplayable. Through the years, I replaced the neck, electronics, pickups, whammy bar, and toggle switch. The only thing that remains from the original instrument is the body and the hippos I drew on it.

Borderline, London, UK. October 23, 1992

“Arm the Homeless” guitar

Whisky A Go Go, Los Angeles. December 13, 1992

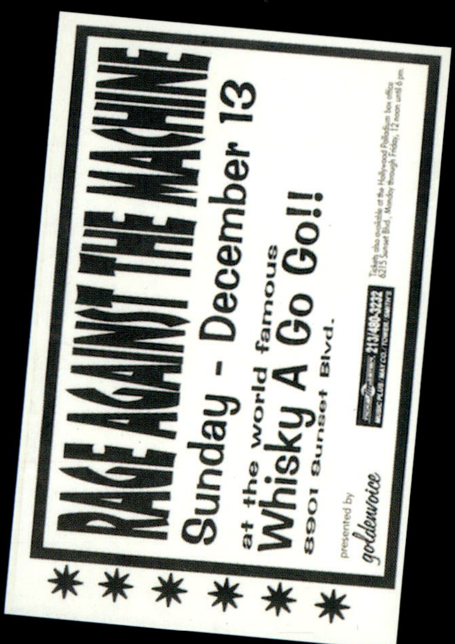

It was exciting to play the Whisky A Go Go. This was where the Doors and Van Halen had played. We always had a really special relationship with our hometown of Los Angeles.

When I first moved to Los Angeles, the Whisky was one of the places I went to see hair bands like Faster Pussycat and Jet Boy. I remember standing in the crowd watching these bands and thinking I could never play like that or look like that, so what chance did we have?

So when we did a show there it was like the world had changed. I wasn't trying on the spandex anymore to look like someone who was in a famous band. I was playing music that I totally believed in.

Pukkelpop, Hasselt, Belgium. August 28, 1993

TOUR DATES

JANUARY 1993

TUE	26	UNDERWORLD	LONDON	ENGLAND
WED	27	BATSCHKAPP	FRANKFURT	GERMANY
THU	28	MARKTHALLE	HAMBURG	GERMANY
FRI	29	OFF	COPENHAGEN	DENMARK
SAT	30	OFF	COPENHAGEN	DENMARK
SUN	31	PUMPEHUSET	COPENHAGEN	DENMARK

FEBRUARY 1993

MON	01	ROCKEFELLER	OSLO	NORWAY
TUE	02	MELODY	STOCKHOLM	SWEDEN
WED	03	TRAVEL		
THU	04	LOFT	BERLIN	GERMANY
FRI	05	"THE WORD" (TV)	LONDON	ENGLAND
SAT	06	V.K.	BRUSSELS	BELGIUM
SUN	07	MELKWEG	AMSTERDAM	HOLLAND
MON	08	ELYSEE MONTMATRE	PARIS	FRANCE
TUE	09	PRESS/TRAVEL		
WED	10	LUXOR	COLOGNE	GERMANY
THU	11	ELECTRIC BALLROOM	ZURICH	SWITZERLAND
FRI	12	CHARTERHALL	MUNICH	GERMANY
SAT	13	ZIMBA	MILAN	ITALY
SUN	14	TRAVEL		
MON	15	TRAVEL		

FEBRUARY CONT...

TUE	16	EDWARDS NO. 8	BIRMINGHAM	ENGLAND
WED	17	ROCK CITY	NOTTINGHAM	ENGLAND
THU	18	PRESS	LONDON	ENGLAND
FRI	19	ULU	LONDON	ENGLAND
SAT	20	TRAVEL		
SUN	21	KING TUT'S	GLASGOW	SCOTLAND
MON	22	BOARDWALK	MANCHESTER	ENGLAND
TUE	23	RIVERSIDE	NEWCASTLE	ENGLAND

Pinkpop, Landgraaf, Netherlands. May 31, 1993

Our next big jump in audience size was the Pinkpop Festival in the Netherlands.

We were late for that show, and we had to go straight from the van onto the stage. We walked out to 60,000 people but didn't even have time to get nervous.

One year later, at Pinkpop 1994, during "Killing in the Name" the crowd registered 1.1 on the Richter scale.

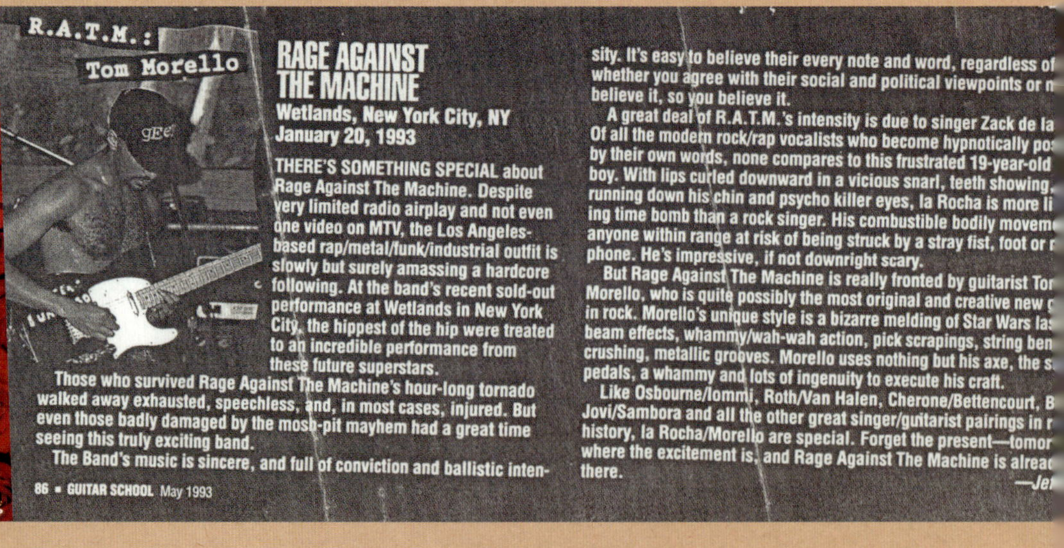

R.A.T.M.: Tom Morello

RAGE AGAINST THE MACHINE

Wetlands, New York City, NY
January 20, 1993

THERE'S SOMETHING SPECIAL about Rage Against The Machine. Despite very limited radio airplay and not even one video on MTV, the Los Angeles-based rap/metal/funk/industrial outfit is slowly but surely amassing a hardcore following. At the band's recent sold-out performance at Wetlands in New York City, the hippest of the hip were treated to an incredible performance from these future superstars.

Those who survived Rage Against The Machine's hour-long tornado walked away exhausted, speechless, and, in most cases, injured. But even those badly damaged by the mosh-pit mayhem had a great time seeing this truly exciting band.

The Band's music is sincere, and full of conviction and ballistic intensity. It's easy to believe their every note and word, regardless of whether you agree with their social and political viewpoints or n believe it, so you believe it.

A great deal of R.A.T.M.'s intensity is due to singer Zack de la Of all the modern rock/rap vocalists who become hypnotically po by their own words, none compares to this frustrated 19-year-old boy. With lips curled downward in a vicious snarl, teeth showing, running down his chin and psycho killer eyes, la Rocha is more li ing time bomb than a rock singer. His combustible bodily movem anyone within range at risk of being struck by a stray fist, foot or phone. He's impressive, if not downright scary.

But Rage Against The Machine is really fronted by guitarist Tor Morello, who is quite possibly the most original and creative new in rock. Morello's unique style is a bizarre melding of Star Wars la beam effects, whammy/wah-wah action, pick scrapings, string ben crushing, metallic grooves. Morello uses nothing but his axe, the s pedals, a whammy and lots of ingenuity to execute his craft.

Like Osbourne/Iommi, Roth/Van Halen, Cherone/Bettencourt, B Jovi/Sambora and all the other great singer/guitarist pairings in r history, la Rocha/Morello are special. Forget the present—tomor where the excitement is, and Rage Against The Machine is alread there.

—Je

86 ▪ GUITAR SCHOOL May 1993

LORI SHEPLER / Los Angeles Times

RAGE FOR CHOICE: In a blistering performance at the Rock for Choice benefit at Hollywood Palladium, Rage Against the Machine, with Zack de la Rocha, confirmed that it has the ambition and vision to stand as the most absorbing L.A. alternative hard-rock band in years. Reviewed by Robert Hilburn. **F1**

POP BEAT

A Night Filled With Sounds of Their Rage

■ Upstart quartet headlines Rock for Choice benefit with music rooted not in peace and love, but in the radicalism of the 1960s.

By ROBERT HILBURN
TIMES POP MUSIC CRITIC

Rage Against the Machine most certainly isn't a band that is afraid of challenges.

On the "Lollapalooza" tour last summer, the upstart Southern California quartet agreed to take the opening spot on the marathon bill.

That meant playing in the hot afternoon sun, a mood-killer that has neutralized the punch of lots of potent groups over the years.

No problem: Rage's blend of furious social commentary and mesmerizing '90s funk-metal stole the day from such alternative rock heroes as Alice in Chains and Primus, even though they benefited from the coolness and dramatic shadings afforded by the darkness.

Headlining the sold-out, seven-act Rock

Please see RAGE, F5

Tour bus

"You can go quietly. Or you can Rock for Choice."

Instead of booking hotels we mostly lived on the bus and it was not high-end accommodation. There are sewers in Calcutta that smell sweeter than the restroom of that bus.

We were all in it together with our lovely, heavy metal road crew of dudes from Wales. In the freezing cold, we would hang our sweaty clothes throughout the bus, which didn't help with the fragrance.

Rock for Choice, Hollywood Palladium, Los Angeles. October 14, 1993

RAGE: Quartet at Palladium

Continued from F1

for Choice benefit on Thursday night at the Hollywood Palladium, Rage faced an even bigger artistic challenge: *following* X and Firehose, two of the most prized acts in Los Angeles alternative-rock history.

Again, no problem.

Rage, which has been together just three years, still hasn't recorded its second Epic album, so it's too early to put the band in the class of X, a group whose quality and integrity set the tone in the early '80s alternative rock scene that also produced such valuable dividends as Los Lobos and the Blasters.

But the Palladium show confirmed that Rage has the ambition and vision to stand as Los Angeles's most absorbing alternative hard-rock arrival in years—possibly since Jane's Addiction in the late '80s.

Despite the obvious ham-fisted implications of its name (only *Down With the Establishment* would be a more literal tag), Rage Against the Machine exhibits considerable individuality and imagination.

At a time in rock when so many groups, from the Spin Doctors to Blind Melon, are wasting our time by recycling the musical earth tones and peace-and-love sentiments associated with the hippie wing of '60s rock, Rage's ideological roots are in '60s radicalism.

Rage's Zack de la Rocha, who combines Chuck D.'s accessibility and fervor as a rapper with Bob Marley's determination and charisma as a performer, doesn't just echo the restless but vague alienation that is the rule among today's new crop of rockers.

The Chicano offers a focus on cultural and social repression that gives his anger more urgency and dimension. In "Take the Power Back," a highlight Thursday, he attacks Eurocentric education tendencies. Sample outcry: *Mother ---- Uncle Sam / Step back / I know who I am.*

His commitment was especially timely at the abortion-rights benefit, which was sponsored by the Feminist Majority Fund and Foundation. Members of the female rock group L7 hosted the concert and David Gunn Jr., the son of slain abortion physician Dr. David Gunn, spoke to the crowd briefly.

But Rage is more than charisma and commentary. In its most intense moments, the band—Timmy C. on bass, Brad Wilk on drums and Tom Morello on guitar—plays with a relentless force that reminds you of grinding machine gears. Yet, there's a precision in the music that sometimes rivals the symphonic grace of Ministry.

Even when De la Rocha does something that doesn't connect (his 10-minute recitation of a favorite poem), you admire his adventurousness.

Firehose, the descendants of the legendary Minutemen and, especially, X, which has been reviewed in these pages recently, played with their usual tenacity, though their brief sets seemed too rushed to document their galvanizing edges. This was Rage's night—and the band didn't flinch.

FAILED
FAILED

Perry Farrell was a huge supporter of the band. He had us open the side stage of Lollapalooza in Los Angeles in 1992 and then the following year he gave us what would be our big break in the United States by inviting us to open the main stage for the whole tour.

When we got to Philadelphia we decided to protest against the PMRC (Parents Music Resource Center), which was a pro-censorship organization founded by Washington senators' wives. They were trying to put warning stickers on heavy metal and rap albums and censor lyrics.

We stood naked on stage for our entire show with "PMRC" duct-taped across our chests. We also had duct tape over our mouths and the only music was guitar feedback.

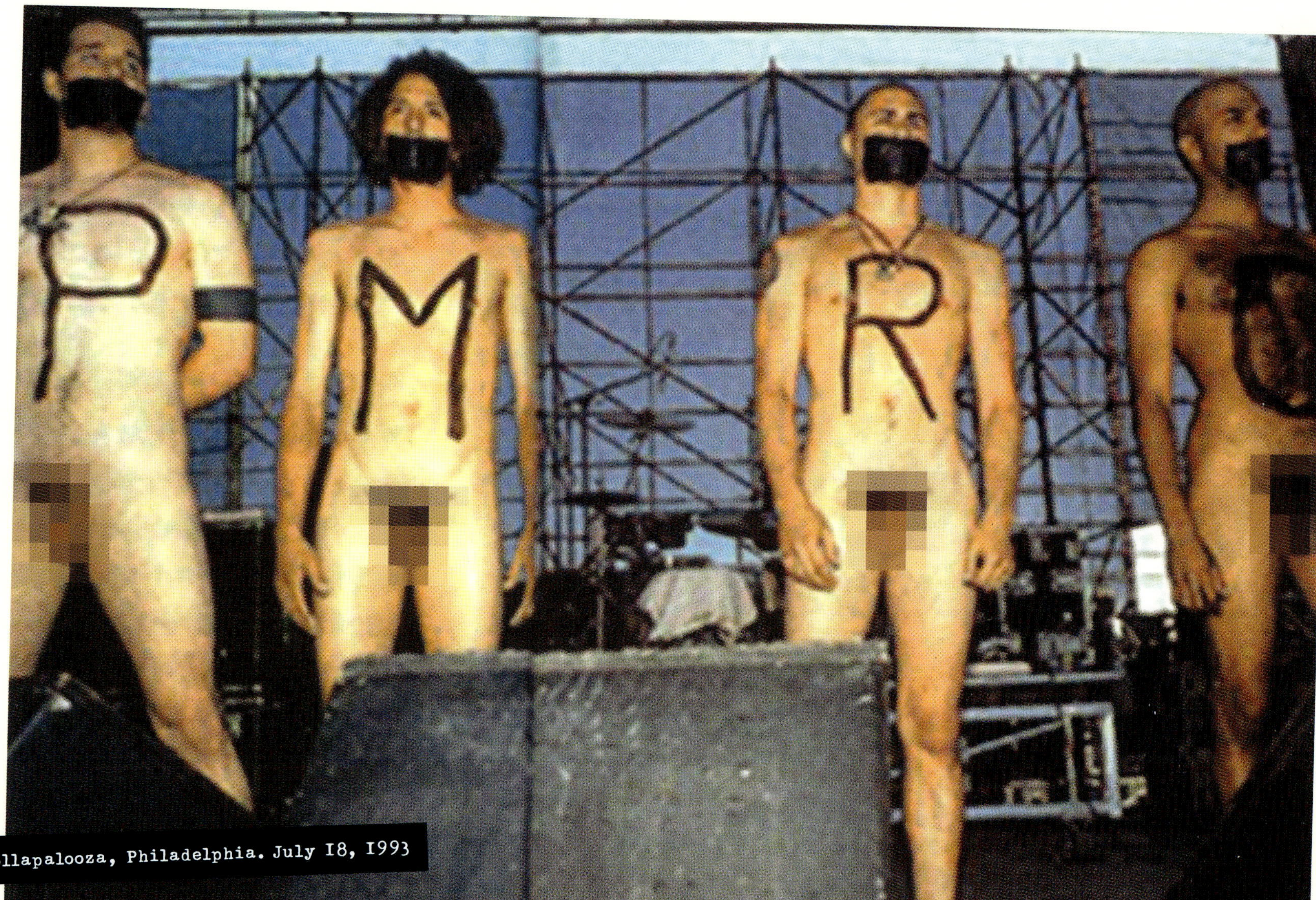

Lollapalooza, Philadelphia. July 18, 1993

For the first five minutes people cheered wildly because they were very excited that Lollapalooza was happening. Then for the next five minutes there was this weird standoff where people were wondering what the hell was going on. For the last five minutes they were booing and throwing quarters at us. Let me tell you, 15 minutes is a long time to be buck naked on stage. That was the amount of time that our tour manager had estimated it would take the cops to get there to arrest us. So that was the length of our set. We walked off stage. No music was played. Boos erupted like crazy. But, we felt that our music was being threatened by people who didn't understand it and didn't understand the First Amendment. We needed to do something, and we sure did.

~~TO~~

I WANT TO THANK THIS BAND

~~THE IS BAND ON~~

~~TODAYS~~ FOR DONATING

THE PROCEEDS OF TODAYS

SHOW TO THE ANTI-CENSORSHIP

ORGANIZATION - PFRR

NOW HERE'S THE BEST

FUCKING BAND ON

LOLLAPALOOZA...

RAGE AGAINST THE MACHINE

PARENTS FOR ROCK AND RAP
P.O. Box 53
Libertyville, IL 60048

WE ADVOCATE:

1. Freedom for artists in the music industry under the first amendment.
2. Parents in charge of their children, not outsiders such as the PMRC, district attorneys, and others.
3. That other problems in the United States must be recognized: poverty, illiteracy, homelessness, joblessness, (we have to keep what we stand for in perspective).
4. Racism is involved as far as 2 Live Crew is concerned. No other albums with similar lyrics have been removed.
5. Eastern Europe is becoming free; we do not want censorship and repression to take over in the United States.

<u>What You Can Do Now:</u>

1. Call the offices of your two Senators and the representative from your district; identify yourself and say you are a member of this organization; ask what the congress-persons stand is on labeling, if the person who answers doesn't know, have them find out and give you a response; if the congress-person is for labeling defend non-labeling(takes artistic freedom away from artists). Also call your state representatives and senators. Deal with them in the same way. They need to know a great number of people do not uphold censorship.

2. Check your local record stores. If they do not have 2 Live Crew's "As Nasty As You Wanna Be", find out the name of the owner of the chain, write them asking that 2 Live Crew's album be put back in the shop. It was put back in Milwaukee and probably other places. If you want to boycott and get your friends to boycott that particular chain do it. Be sure in whatever you do you mention that you are a member of this organization. There is power in numbers.

F ... t

My mother founded Parents for Rock and Rap, an anti-censorship organization, as a counterweight to the PMRC.

SOUNDOFF!

MUSICIANS AGAINST CENSORSH

"...Elites seek to rule and impose social stability by the application of 'traditional values'—of authority, profit, family hierarchy, moral rigidity and class domination."

The Nation, February 11, 1991

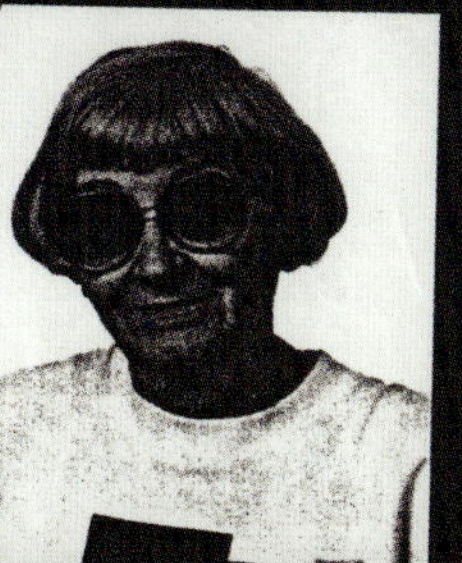

Parents for Rock and Rap was formed as a counter-force to Parents Music Resource Center and some of the fundamentalists who attempt to control people's lives. In the United States, freedom is guaranteed to every citizen by the first amendment. As one of our members wrote when he joined (a father, a U.S. Army sergeant, stationed in Berlin), "The first amendment is not negotiable." PFRR works for freedom of expression for artists in the music industry, but we cross over into all of the arts if and when necessary. Our organization includes not just parents, but anyone interested in fighting censorship and repression of musicians. Music censorship consists of record labeling, either self-imposed or legally mandated, communities regulating which artists may or may not perform, age restrictions on concert goers and record buyers, and record stores refusing to store certain "objectionable" albums.

Censorship is on the rise. Contradictory to what the far right says, the majority of Americans want their arts to be free. PFRR members include: students of all ages, parents, grandparents, college professors, representatives of news media, lawyers, veterans, artists in the music industry, rock, rap and metal, writers, editors, ad infinitum. PFRR is beginning to have power and clout because at the present time we have hundreds of active members in the United States, Canada, England, Germany and even one member from Nigeria. We keep growing.

The purpose of our organization is to target any censorship of artists in the music industry. We work as a total organization, or the seventeen regional representatives work with their members, or we work individually. We call Congresspeople, governors, assembly people, record chains, write letters when there is censorship. When something happens in your area you have many options. If the problem is a city board regulating who can and cannot view a concert, or which groups can or cannot perform in your community, attend board meetings and protest (call your municipal building to find out when and where they are held). If there is police harassment during or after a concert you can call the chief of police to protest, contact the mayor of the community, write letters to the editors of the local papers. If you think your state legislature or Congress is attempting to censor, the Congress opinion number is (202) 224-3121; ask the operator for a specific Senator or Representative. You have a state assembly person representing the area where you live. Find out who it is and contact them with your opinion. Type up a petition, get signatures, send it to the person or persons involved. Write and call record store owners and owners of other chains and tell them you will boycott their shops if they continue to practice censorship. Write record company presidents who attempt to censor their own artists.

I must mention my great disappointment with record companies and artists who have succumbed to the pressure of censorship. Not all! The owners of record companies have enough money and clout that they could have fought the labeling and won, especially since they have the first amendment on their side.

This brings us around to parents. Parents, not the government nor outside forces, should help their children make decisions. Parents have to realize that they don't belong to the generation their children have joined, just as they were different from their parents' generation. They can listen to their children's albums and discuss the lyrics if they don't approve. Many parents would not think of interfering in their young person's choice of music. They look upon music as a good outlet. Parents should love their children, give them what advice they can and set them free. If they falter be there for them. Parental neglect and abuse is a far worse and damaging problem for young people.

I want to at least mention the racism that has always entered the picture when Afro-Americans are involved. Those who are white, bigoted parents resent their young enjoying the music of Afro-Americans. The negativism against rap was and is pure racism. Look at the clone someone came up with to counter the influence of those who would bring social issues before the American public.

You don't have to be a teenager to be alarmed by music censorship. I am 67 years old and the mother of a rock musician. I do not have money nor am I famous but I am never frightened of any opposition. I believe an artist is not an artist if he or she is not free to express herself or himself in an art. Whether we enjoy rap or rock, reggae or even country music, as Americans, if we are to be free, we have to fight against censorship and to uphold the first amendment.

Peace

Mary Morello
Parents for Rock and Rap
PO Box 53
Libertyville, IL 60048

MUSICIAN
Where the Players Do the Talking™

Parents go on record: Don't curb rap 'n' roll

By Gary Wisby

Watch out, Tipper Gore. Here comes Mary Morello.

Morello, a 66-year-old retired schoolteacher from Libertyville who's almost too tolerant to be true, has formed Parents for Rock and Rap, a nationwide anti-censorship group.

So far, 200 people have joined, "and it hasn't even been going a month," she said.

Morello was inspired by her son, a rock 'n' roll musician, and by Tipper Gore, an advocate of music censorship and wife of Sen. Albert Gore Jr. (D-Tenn.).

Three years ago at a PTA meeting, Morella saw a video produced by Gore's group, the Parents' Music Resource Center, which campaigns against music it deems obscene.

Since she believes in the First Amendment, and since she had never been bothered by her son's high school heavy metal band, which practiced in her basement, Morello spoke up against censoring music. Her remarks drew applause from parents, including some with kids in rock bands, and gave birth to her anti-censorship group.

"We advocate parents being in charge of their children, rather than some outside organization," said Morello. "If they bring a tape home and you don't want them to have it, you throw it away."

Her group has had "tremendous response" and she has members in 35 states, she said. "I love the letters from kids who've studied the Constitution," said Morello, who taught African studies, world history and American history in her 22 years at Libertyville High School.

In fact, it was her teaching career that helped her "put up with just about anything," said Morello.

What's her opinion of the controversial rap group 2 Live Crew, whose album was labeled obscene and banned in Florida?

"We back their freedom under the First Amendment, of course," said Morello, who had "no comment" on their lyrics.

She did say, "A lot of white Americans don't understand black culture. . . . I like rap and I wish I knew more about it."

Tom Morello, 26, plays in a Los Angeles-based band called Lock-Up. He said he and his mom have traded influences: "She introduced me to Stevie Wonder and the Temptations, and I returned the favor by introducing her to Jimi Hendrix and Led Zeppelin."

SUN-TIMES/Nancy Stuenkel

Mary Morello, retired Libertyville schoolteacher and founder of the new anti-censorship group, Parents for Rock and Rap, holds a photo of her son Tom, 26, in his Los Angeles band, Lock-Up.

I bought the "Creamy" guitar for 40 Canadian dollars at a pawn shop in Toronto. I don't even know what it's made of. Possibly plywood. I play it on "Tire Me," the song for which we won our first Grammy in 1996. None of the knobs on it work.

"Creamy" guitar

Often when practicing I would come up with a brand new sound, and a day later forget how I made it. Enter the Noise Chart. When experimenting with new and exotic sounds I would immediately record them on my little RadioShack cassette recorder and then write the details of which knobs, pedals, and techniques were used to create that sound. From helicopter rotor blades to barnyard animal sounds, once they were on the Noise Chart I wasn't going to forget them.

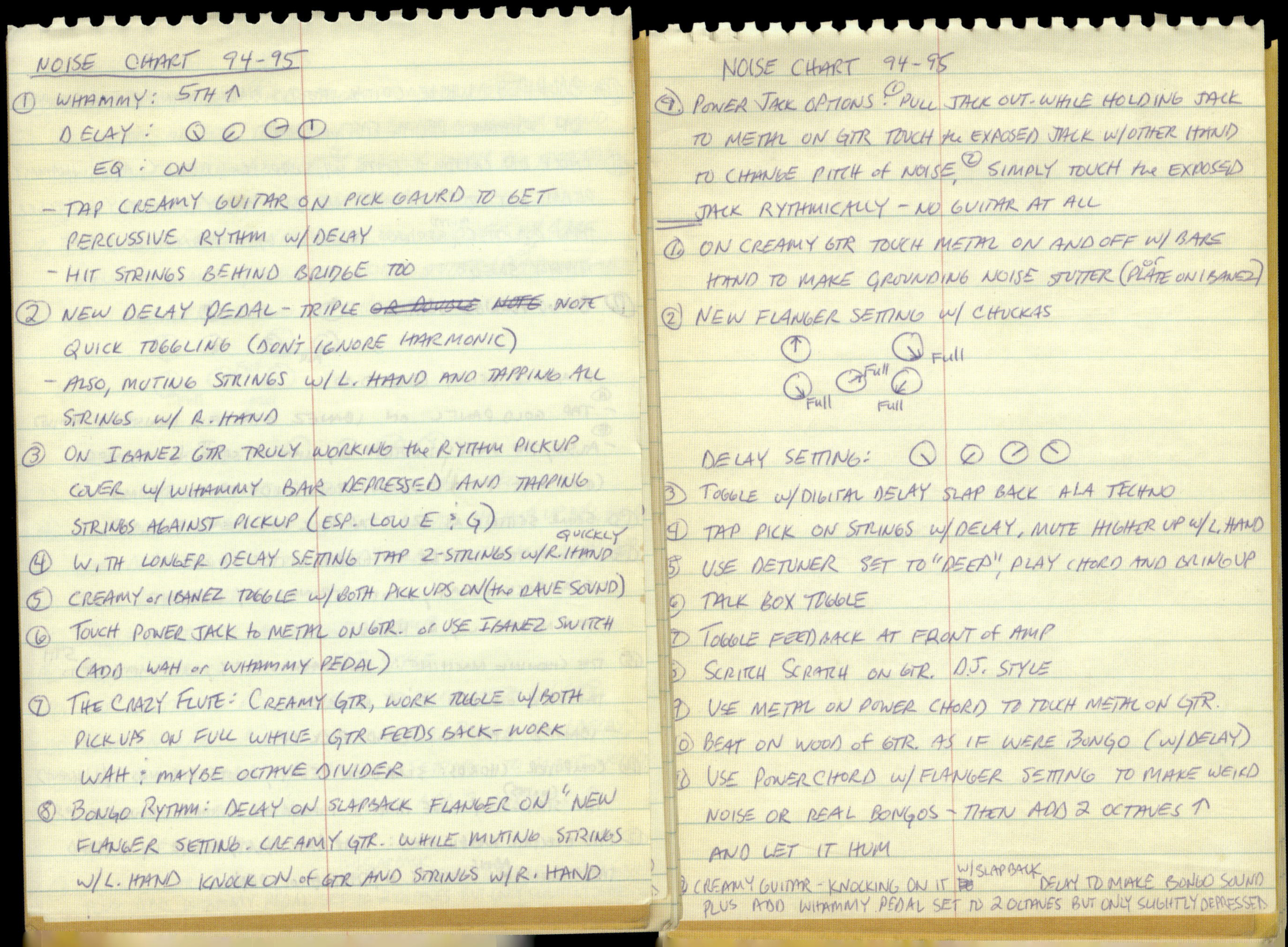

NOISE CHART 94-95

① WHAMMY: 5TH ↑
DELAY:
EQ: ON
- TAP CREAMY GUITAR ON PICK GAURD TO GET PERCUSSIVE RYTHM W/DELAY
- HIT STRINGS BEHIND BRIDGE TOO

② NEW DELAY PEDAL - TRIPLE ~~OR DOUBLE NOTE~~ NOTE QUICK TOGGLING (DON'T IGNORE HARMONIC)
- ALSO, MUTING STRINGS W/ L. HAND AND TAPPING ALL STRINGS W/ R. HAND

③ ON IBANEZ GTR TRULY WORKING the RYTHM PICKUP COVER W/WHAMMY BAR DEPRESSED AND TAPPING STRINGS AGAINST PICKUP (ESP. LOW E & G)

④ WITH LONGER DELAY SETTING TAP 2-STRINGS QUICKLY W/R. HAND

⑤ CREAMY or IBANEZ TOGGLE W/ BOTH PICK UPS ON (the RAVE SOUND)

⑥ TOUCH POWER JACK to METAL ON GTR. or USE IBANEZ SWITCH (ADD WAH or WHAMMY PEDAL)

⑦ THE CRAZY FLUTE: CREAMY GTR, WORK TOGGLE W/BOTH PICKUPS ON FULL WHILE GTR FEEDS BACK - WORK WAH & MAYBE OCTAVE DIVIDER

⑧ BONGO RYTHM: DELAY ON SLAPBACK FLANGER ON "NEW FLANGER SETTING". CREAMY GTR. WHILE MUTING STRINGS W/L. HAND KNOCK ON of GTR AND STRINGS W/R. HAND

NOISE CHART 94-95

⑨ POWER JACK OPTIONS: ① PULL JACK OUT. WHILE HOLDING JACK TO METAL ON GTR TOUCH the EXPOSED JACK W/OTHER HAND TO CHANGE PITCH of NOISE, ② SIMPLY TOUCH the EXPOSED JACK RYTHMICALLY - NO GUITAR AT ALL

① ON CREAMY GTR TOUCH METAL ON AND OFF W/ BARE HAND TO MAKE GROUNDING NOISE STUTTER (or PLATE ON IBANEZ)

② NEW FLANGER SETTING W/ CHUCKAS
Full Full Full Full

DELAY SETTING:

③ TOGGLE W/DIGITAL DELAY SLAP BACK ALA TECHNO

④ TAP PICK ON STRINGS W/DELAY, MUTE HIGHER UP W/L. HAND

⑤ USE DETUNER SET TO "DEEP", PLAY CHORD AND BRING UP

⑥ TALK BOX TOGGLE

⑦ TOGGLE FEEDBACK AT FRONT of AMP

⑧ SCRITCH SCRATCH ON GTR. D.J. STYLE

⑨ USE METAL ON POWER CHORD TO TOUCH METAL ON GTR.

⑩ BEAT ON WOOD of GTR. AS IF WERE BONGO (W/DELAY)

⑪ USE POWERCHORD W/FLANGER SETTING TO MAKE WEIRD NOISE OR REAL BONGOS - THEN ADD 2 OCTAVES ↑ AND LET IT HUM

⑫ CREAMY GUITAR - KNOCKING ON IT W/SLAPBACK DELAY TO MAKE BONGO SOUND PLUS ADD WHAMMY PEDAL SET TO 2 OCTAVES BUT ONLY SLIGHTLY DEPRESSED

The Leonard Peltier benefit concert at the Cal State Dominguez Hills Velodrome was a very important night—at the time our biggest headlining show.

The opening act, Beastie Boys, came out in UPS suits, played ten of their biggest bangers in a row, and destroyed the place. We opened with a 14-minute-long Allen Ginsberg poem and a lot of deep cuts, which were met with relative indifference. It was an important lesson that informed every set list I've ever written from that day forward.

Leonard Peltier benefit, Carson, CA. April 29, 1994

Mumia Abu-Jamal benefit, Washington, DC. August 13, 1995

Left to right: Tom Morello, Zack de la Rocha, Adam Yauch, Tim Commerford, Brad Wilk

The following year we held the first of our two benefit events to try to free the political prisoner Mumia Abu-Jamal.

The Beastie Boys played that show, too, which was the first time we had seen them since the Leonard Peltier benefit. This time I was ready—I'd been working on the set list for three months. I saw Mike D before the show. I said, "Hey, so what are you guys playing tonight?" I looked over his shoulder and he had made a set list in alphabetical order! He just thought, "Let's do the songs in alphabetical order—that'll be fun." So it wasn't exactly the grudge match I was expecting, and we had a good laugh.

Tibetan Freedom Concert, San Francisco. June 16, 1996

We've played a couple of Tibetan Freedom Concerts through the years to support Adam Yauch and the Beastie Boys.

Rock Werchter Festival, Werchter, Belgium. July 6, 1996

We recorded the entire *Evil Empire* album in Los Angeles at Cole Rehearsal Studios, a tiny, weather-beaten spot. With producer Brendan O'Brien, we just rocked those songs in that small room with no separation between the instruments. That's how we captured the raw intensity of *Evil Empire*.

Cole Studios

Here, we are rehearsing the song "Revolver." The intro has a sound that evokes "the forest coming to life" which was created with this custom-made Ibanez guitar.

Saturday Night Live Thursday night rehearsal with Steve Forbes before everything went to hell.

NBC Studios, New York City. April II, 1996

The week *Evil Empire* came out, we played *Saturday Night Live* and the host was Steve Forbes, the billionaire former presidential candidate. It was all very ironic. We had upside-down American flags as part of our regular stage backdrop. NBC said we couldn't do that because it would be offensive to their sponsors and to the host. We winked and agreed to take them down.

I suppose they forgot that our most famous song has a refrain that goes, "Fuck you, I won't do what you tell me." So a minute before we went live, our roadies put the flags back up. The NBC stage manager ordered us to take them down. A brawl erupted on stage between our crew and their crew. They managed to rip off the upside-down flags moments before Steve Forbes introduced the band.

NBC politely told us that they "didn't have time for our second song that night" and they would like to escort us to the sidewalk. That week, we had the Number One album in the US, which was unheard of for a band with our sound and politics.

Radio Free LA, January 20, 1997

On inauguration night of 1997, we hosted Radio Free LA, a global broadcast featuring incendiary performances by Cypress Hill, and Beck, and a short set by Zack, Flea, Stephen Perkins, and myself. The show also featured interviews with political prisoners, Native American activist Leonard Peltier, Mumia Abu-Jamal (from death row), Noam Chomsky, Subcomandante Marcos of the Zapatistas, Michael Moore, and radical Santa Monica High School students.

Troubador, Los Angeles. January 23, 1999

The Battle of Los Angeles was also recorded with Brendan O'Brien. We finished it a day before appearing at Woodstock '99. *Rolling Stone*, *Spin*, and *Time* magazine all dubbed it Album of the Year for 1999. Upon completing the album, we went straight to Japan.

Woodstock '99, Rome, NY. July 24, 1999

Rolling Stone cover shoot, 1999

CLASS WAR
JUST DO IT.
LIBERTYVILLE
ARM THE HOMELESS
KODAK 5052 TMX
KODAK TMX 6052

The first time I met Michael Moore was on the day of the "Sleep Now in the Fire" video shoot, which he was directing. I was a huge fan of his confrontational filmmaking and I couldn't wait to ask him how many times he'd been arrested. He surprised me by answering, "Never." I jokingly said, "Well, you've never worked with Rage Against the Machine."

We were filming on Wall Street and the video shoot was wild. It began with the band predicting Donald Trump's presidency (apologies) and ended with capitalism briefly grinding to a halt on a Tuesday afternoon as the riot doors slammed shut on the New York Stock Exchange. Also, Michael Moore was arrested.

The protest gig outside the 2000 Democratic National Convention in Los Angeles turned into a huge police riot when our crowd was attacked by the cops. There were countless injuries and arrests. We had put out a record called *The Battle of Los Angeles* and then it manifested before our eyes.

Democratic National Convention, Los Angeles. August 14, 2000

I love the idea of the guitar being a visual as well as a musical extension of the artist. It's one more canvas that you can paint on.

Maynard Keenan of Tool taught me how to play drop D tuning but I couldn't do it on my "Arm the Homeless" guitar because it has a locking nut. My roommate at the time, Scott Tracy, had an extra guitar, a Fender Telecaster. I traded him an amp for his Telecaster and this became my principal guitar for all the drop D songs henceforth.

The Telecaster has a single coil pickup and has helped me to find a unique sound when writing riffs.

"Sendero Luminoso" Fender Telecaster

About half the songs on the first Rage album are in drop D tuning, including "Killing in the Name" and "Freedom." The Audioslave song "Show Me How to Live" also employs drop D tuning, which provides a distinctive way to play barre chords.

In October 2000, we recorded two nights at the Grand Olympic Auditorium in Los Angeles for a live album. They were powerful shows and turned out to be the last Rage Against the Machine shows for a long time.

It was electric, and when we were on stage there was a punk rock fury that was tangible. Our musical chemistry came from that unique combination of four people who produced something none of us could have created with anyone else.

Grand Olympic Auditorium, Los Angeles. September, 2000

Our last studio album, *Renegades*, was produced by Rick Rubin. Originally, we were just intending to record a couple of cover songs as bonus tracks for the *Live at the Grand Olympic Auditorium* album, but soon those recordings began to feel like an album in their own right.

Although *Renegades* is a covers album, the music is all original. So in some ways it's an original Rage Against the Machine record built around the lyrical touchstones of artists we respect.

Rick's a genius producer, good friend, and a cruel taskmaster. You would finish a take and you'd be psyched. As the cymbals died away, everyone would be very, very quiet because that was certainly *the* take! And then you'd look in the control room and Rick would be holding his nose with a thumb down, disgusted. "Damn it, Rick!"

Rick's become a lifelong friend and during that period we were hanging out every day like an old married couple.

Coachella, Indio, CA. April 29, 2007

Rage Against the Machine reformed at Coachella in April 2007.

I remember getting ready to walk onto the stage and the anticipation out there was like an ocean of gasoline waiting for a match. As we were walking toward the stage, I heard a guy in the little tented area backstage saying, "Holy shit, it's really going to happen!" And that set me thinking, "Holy shit, it's really going to happen!"

We returned to the festival scene and the shows were just incredible. Some people had never had the chance to see Rage Against the Machine; others remembered us well. We owned our headliner status and we wanted to fulfill that level of expectation.

Voodoo Music Experience Festival, New Orleans. October 26, 2007

We did the shows with the Wu-Tang Clan on the Rock the Bells hip-hop tour, which were pretty amazing.

T in the Park, Balado, Scotland, UK. July 12, 2008

There were no pyrotechnics, just the red star behind us. Four guys on stage. We turned the lights on, and the crowd jumped up and down. That was the whole show, and that was more than enough.

Pinkpop, Landgraaf, Netherlands. June 1, 2008

We had a new sense of purpose and commitment. At Pinkpop Festival we dressed in Guantanamo Bay-style prison uniforms.

Reading Festival, Reading, UK. August 25, 2008

Democratic National Convention, Denver. August 27, 2008

We performed at protests surrounding the Democratic and Republican conventions. The cops pulled the plug on our show at the 2008 Republican National Convention in Minneapolis, so we carried on with a bullhorn in the middle of the crowd.

Republican National Convention, Minneapolis. September 3, 2008

Slim Richardson had been my guitar tech since 1992.

RollingStone

100 Greatest Guitarists

26

Tom Morello

In the early days of Rage Against the Machine, Morello watched local California metal guitarists play "as fast as Yngwie Malmsteen" and realized, "That wasn't a race I wanted to run." So he began to experiment with the toggle switch on his guitar to produce an effect like a DJ scratching a record. The result was true rap metal and a redefinition of the guitar's potential. Morello absorbs hip-hop mixology as a true son of Grandmaster Flash and the Voodoo Child, making his riffs rumble and boom like crosstown turntable traffic.

I did not expect that becoming an avatar in *Guitar Hero III: Legends of Rock* would impact my life the way that it did. My fan demographic began including five-year-olds and regularly jackasses would approach me on the street and proudly proclaim, "I kicked your ass at *Guitar Hero*, man!"

Unexpectedly, in 2009 Rage Against the Machine had the UK Christmas Number One pop song.

For the previous five years the winner of Simon Cowell's *X Factor* talent show had held that honor. A suburban London couple launched a social media campaign to suggest that "Killing in the Name," then 17 years old, would make a better Number One. Against all odds, a popular groundswell of support pushed our song to the top of the charts, with the most singles downloaded in one week in UK chart history.

To celebrate, we promised we'd put on a free show in the UK. The capacity at Finsbury Park was supposed to be 45,000 people, but 90,000 attended the concert and it remains one of my favorite rock 'n' roll moments ever.

Finsbury Park free gig, London, UK. June 6, 2010

RATM

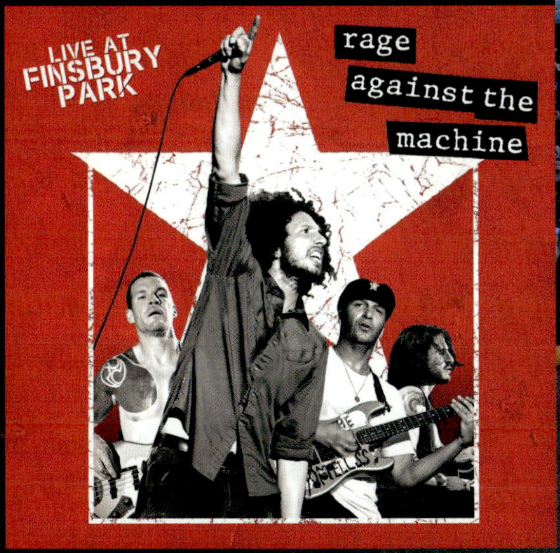
LIVE AT
FINSBURY
PARK
rage
against the
machine

The Battle of Santiago and the Finsbury Park UK show were two of the craziest crowds I've ever seen in my life.

We played a benefit at the Hollywood Palladium to support Arizona organizations combating the SB 1070 law, a racist immigration policy. It's a band that still has work to do.

Hollywood Palladium, Los Angeles. June 23, 2010

OCT 28, PHILLY

YOUR TIME HAS COME Soul

SET IT OFF Soul

DOESN'T REMIND ME ~~Soul~~ HIP

OUT OF EXILE Tele

CAPO → BE YOURSELF CAPO Soul

RUSTY CAGE LP '3'

SPOONMAN RED

LIGHT MY WAY Tele

MAN OR ANIMAL BARI

LIKE A STONE SOUL

60'S JAM Tele

BULLS/SLEEP NOW HIP

SHADOW LP '3'

BLACK HOLE SUN

HIGHWAY HIP

SHOW ME HOW TO LIVE Tele

KILLING IN THE NAME Tele

COCHISE Soul

Audioslave

First Audioslave photo shoot with our good friend photographer Danny Clinch in downtown Los Angeles

In the aftermath of the Rage Against the Machine breakup in late 2000, Tim and Brad and I spent a lot of time over at Rick Rubin's house brainstorming, talking about people we'd like to work with and listening to records. One album we kept coming back to was Soundgarden's *Badmotorfinger*. Chris Cornell's beautiful and terrifyingly powerful voice was just chilling. We approached him about jamming together and at the first session we wrote "Light My Way." Audioslave was born.

Rick Rubin told us, "I work with a million singers and what Chris Cornell does, being able to create melody like that, is very, very special."

New band, new guitar. It was very important for me to recast my guitar playing for Audioslave. I found a cool Fender Stratocaster that I modified by putting a toggle switch and a hot-rail pickup on it, which gave it its own very original sound.

I remember the day I got the guitar. I went straight home and wrote "Soul Power" on it. It was going to be my divining rod to explore new sounds. There was a tremendous amount of love and soul in the room when we were writing those songs.

Audioslave began with a tremendous burst of creativity and renewed artistic vigor. Chris's incredible voice led us into uncharted musical territory and that debut album remains one of the favorites of my career.

The "Cochise" video was lit entirely by fireworks. We shot it in the San Fernando Valley and people called the cops. They thought it was a terrorist attack.

Every day, Tim would come up with something, Brad would come up with something, and I would come up with something. Chris's unique ability was that he could craft incredible melodies around whatever you threw at him. Whether it was a complicated, rolling thunder riff or a three-chord progression, he could make a great song out of it.

Storm Thorgerson, the famed Pink Floyd album designer, had an idea for the album cover. Storm created a huge golden fire sculpture and transported it to Iceland for this photo. That's him standing in front of it. He was a very eccentric and wonderful guy.

Our first live performance was on top of the Ed Sullivan Theater in New York City.

It was a strange place for a debut gig, but I've always believed that if you have the confidence in yourself and your band mates, it doesn't matter if you are playing in front of 60,000 people, or in a small club, or on the marquee of the Ed Sullivan Theater, you'll be alright.

There was a big crowd on the street, but there was also an office building opposite. All of the windows were open and people kept shouting, "Chris, take your shirt off!"

The Late Show with David Letterman,
Ed Sullivan Theater, New York City. November 25, 2002

It was great to be in our hometown with an exciting new band and a record that we loved.

LA debut, KROQ Almost Acoustic Christmas. December 7, 2002

We had a lot of chordal ideas that Chris navigated like the brilliant rock god that he was. It was exciting and the music we made had both beauty and ferocity.

inconsistent
rerecord 10 songs

- Shakers, percussion
- arrangements almost there
- Geto Boys not Chili Peppers

Recommends Against remixing
Tape doesn't capture how good the band is.
Continuity
$ better spent - ferocious

Warfield Theatre, San Francisco, CA. March 19, 2003

Pinkpop, Landgraaf, Netherlands. June 9, 2003

One thing the "Soul Power" guitar uniquely did for me was provide a really broad sonic spectrum: from the soft strumming chords of "Doesn't Remind Me," or the little jangling melody of "Be Yourself" to the pure fury of "Cochise." It pushed me in other directions, to think in different ways about melody, riffs and about crazy noises.

The video for "Show Me How To Live" was inspired by the film *Vanishing Point*, a favorite of Chris Cornell. We recreated clips from the 70's outlaw flick in which a renegade in a 1970 Dodge Challenger eludes the law on a defiant but ultimately doomed mission.

"Show Me How To Live" video shoot, 2003

Lollapalooza. July-August, 2003

Backstage at Lollapalooza, Indianapolis. July 5, 2003

For the first tour we only played Audioslave songs and a couple of cover songs. We really wanted to establish the band as its own entity. We thought we had made a strong enough record and, while our audience followed us from our previous bands, it was important to be Audioslave right off the bat.

Here I am working the knobs on my original Digitech Whammy pedal, which I've had since 1991.

Lollapalooza. July-August, 2003

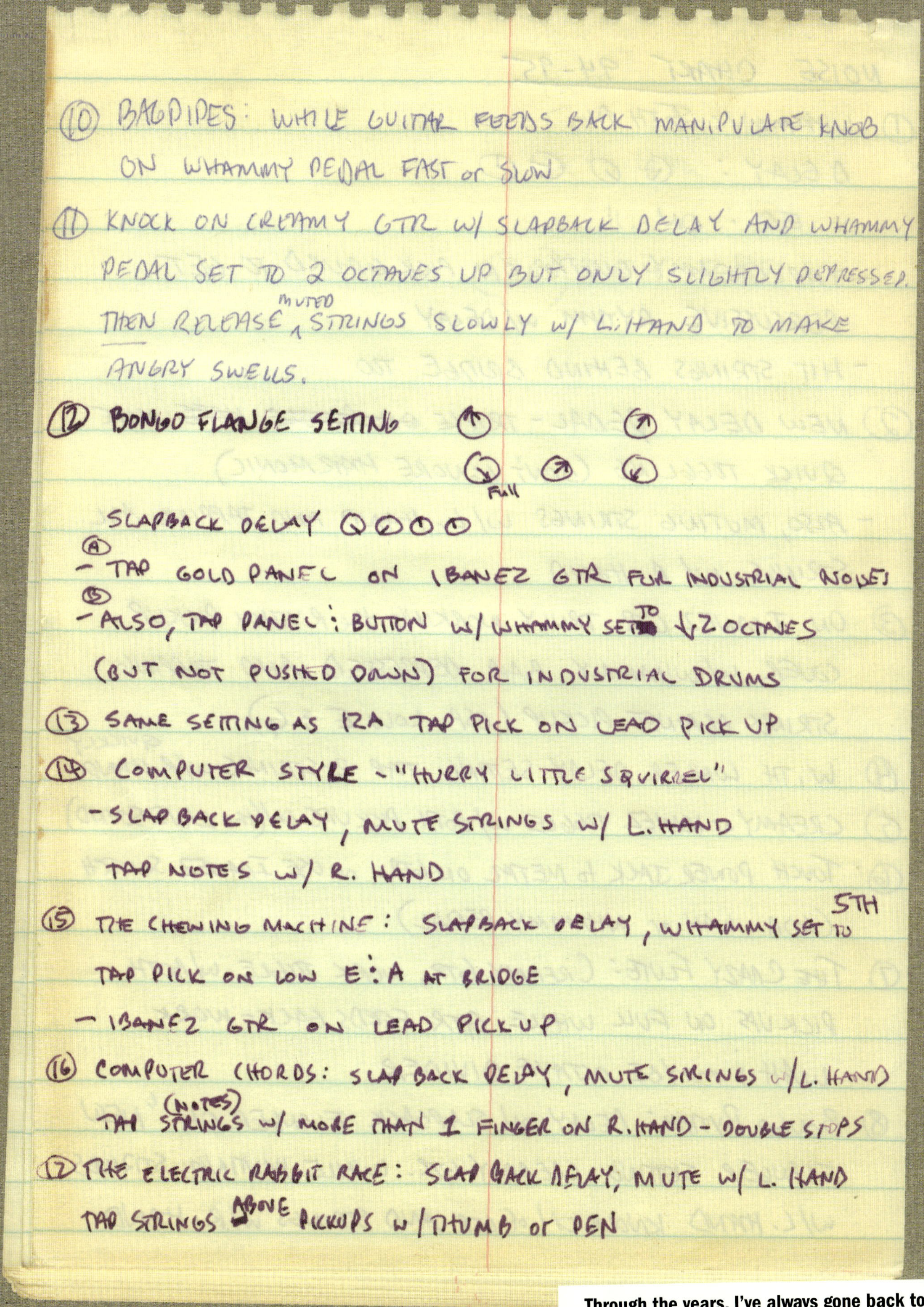

(10) BAGPIPES: WHILE GUITAR FEEDS BACK MANIPULATE KNOB ON WHAMMY PEDAL FAST or SLOW

(11) KNOCK ON CREAMY GTR W/ SLAPBACK DELAY AND WHAMMY PEDAL SET TO 2 OCTAVES UP BUT ONLY SLIGHTLY DEPRESSED. THEN RELEASE MUTED STRINGS SLOWLY W/ L. HAND TO MAKE ANGRY SWELLS.

(12) BONGO FLANGE SETTING

Full

SLAPBACK DELAY

(A) - TAP GOLD PANEL ON IBANEZ GTR FOR INDUSTRIAL NOISES

(B) - ALSO, TAP PANEL & BUTTON W/ WHAMMY SET TO ↓2 OCTAVES (BUT NOT PUSHED DOWN) FOR INDUSTRIAL DRUMS

(13) SAME SETTING AS 12A TAP PICK ON LEAD PICK UP

(14) COMPUTER STYLE - "HURRY LITTLE SQUIRREL"

- SLAPBACK DELAY, MUTE STRINGS W/ L. HAND
TAP NOTES W/ R. HAND

(15) THE CHEWING MACHINE: SLAPBACK DELAY, WHAMMY SET TO 5TH
TAP PICK ON LOW E & A AT BRIDGE

- IBANEZ GTR ON LEAD PICKUP

(16) COMPUTER CHORDS: SLAPBACK DELAY, MUTE STRINGS W/ L. HAND
TAP STRINGS (NOTES) W/ MORE THAN 1 FINGER ON R. HAND - DOUBLE STOPS

(17) THE ELECTRIC RABBIT RACE: SLAPBACK DELAY, MUTE W/ L. HAND
TAP STRINGS ABOVE PICKUPS W/ THUMB or PEN

Through the years, I've always gone back to my Noise Chart for inspiration.

Audioslave was the first American rock band to play in Cuba.

Cuba Free Concert, Havana. May 6, 2005

It came about after an 18-month negotiation between the US Treasury Department and the Cuban Ministry of Culture. It was incredible. We broke the rock 'n' roll blockade of Cuba.

The deal was that it would be a cultural exchange. We weren't allowed to sell tickets so Cuba's part of the exchange was for us to spend three or four days visiting a jazz school, a museum in a fort, and hanging out along the Malecón, Havana's seafront, jamming with local musicians. Our part of the bargain was that we played a free show at the José Martí Anti-Imperialist Platform.

There was no promoter so we had no idea how many people would even come. So on a few of the nights before the show my wife and I went to bars and handed out fliers. It turned out we didn't need to: 70,000 people showed up.

Cuba Free Concert, Havana. May 6, 2005

It was actually my second time in Cuba. I had been there once less legally for about a month.

People warned me that my room was going to be bugged. But really it's just like going to Jamaica without the commercial pornography of billboards screaming at you. And there's no trace of the Kardashians. They've endured a US blockade for more than 50 years now, so they don't have PlayStations and the latest iPhones. Instead, people play chess in the street. They freestyle to acoustic guitars along the Malecón. There's this richness in culture, and pride in their differentness from—and continued defiance toward—the United States.

Fields of Rock, Nijmegen, Netherlands. May 18, 2005

KROQ Weenie Roast, Los Angeles. May 21, 2005

The *Out of Exile* record was produced by Rick Rubin and mixed by Brendan O'Brien. We embarked on an arena tour and began incorporating Rage, Soundgarden, and Temple of Doom songs in our set.

Jimmy Kimmel Live!, Los Angeles. May 18, 2005

In Audioslave, in order to achieve the harmonic interplay that would allow Chris to soar as a vocalist, we continued to push ourselves musically.

Brixton Academy, London, UK. June 19, 2005

Ibanez Talman with custom Kenyan flag artwork

funky song
IPB
Rock Jam
Corneillan jam
Big Beat
Gold
Wilk Rock
Wrecking Ball
Ending Wrecking Ball
Metalistone
Japanese melody
Mystery Jam
60's Jam
Nuno in D
Hip hop

Working song titles for *Revelations* demos

We were embracing our legacies as well as the new sound we were crafting.

The first time I played Madison Square Garden was with Audioslave. I'm a huge fan of Led Zeppelin's concert film *The Song Remains the Same*, which was filmed there. To be in that same room in front of a sold-out crowd playing those riffs on my humble Telecaster felt pretty great.

When the third record, *Revelations*, came out Audioslave had already broken up. It really felt like we were finding our own voice and this album pointed to a new kind of rock band and a new direction. But we went our separate ways.

Madison Square Garden, New York City. October 29, 2005

This was a Budweiser promotional guitar that had shown up in a dressing room, and I hadn't bothered to throw it away or give it away.

One night I looked at this poor woebegone guitar tucked at the end of my rack. It was the end of the day and everyone was going home. I took Chris's lighter, went out to the parking lot, and burned off the Budweiser logo and then it looked kind of cool.

I just kept burning it and I took some steel wool and sanded it down. Suddenly it looked good, but it still didn't sound very good. I gave it to my guitar tech and said, "Give me whatever pickups Ace Frehley used on the *Kiss Alive!* record. Put those in there, fix the neck, and hand that thing back to me." And then it became the main guitar for a lot of the songs on *Revelations*.

FIGHT! SMASH! WIN!

SOMEWHERE IN THE WORLD IT'S MIDNIGHT

PAPER PLANES

THE OATH

100 LITTLE CURSES

PROMENADE

NOBODY MOVES (TIL WE SAY GO)

Street Sweeper Social Club

When Audioslave broke up, Boots Riley and I had dinner and I didn't give him a choice. I said, "We're in a band called Street Sweeper Social Club," and gave him a cassette tape of 24 song ideas and said, "Here's the music. You'll write lyrics and we'll make a record."

NINJA tour, Clarkston, MI. May 31, 2009

We were always well dressed in Street Sweeper Social Club.

Boots Riley was once best known for being the rapper in a group called the Coup. He's now a hot indie film director, having written and directed the 2018 movie *Sorry to Bother You*. I just thought he was such a charismatic performer and brilliant lyricist.

KROQ's Epicenter Festival, Pomona, CA. September 22, 2009

There's a very short list of people who, when you ask them to play a benefit show, they always say yes. Boots is on that list.

Jail Guitar Doors launch, Austin, TX. 2010

MC5 founder Wayne Kramer runs an organization called Jail Guitar Doors that provides musical instruments as rehabilitation tools in penitentiaries. We would perform in the prisons, and then we'd leave the instruments behind. Giving inmates an outlet to express themselves through music dramatically impacts the recidivism rate and I consider Brother Wayne Kramer a real hero.

Tom Morello Becomes First Musician to be Named ACLU 'Smart Justice' Ambassador

COURAGE CAMPAIGN TO HONOR LEGENDARY GUITARIST TOM MORELLO AT SPIRIT OF COURAGE AWARDS

National Air Traffic Controllers Union
Noted labor activist and musician Tom Morello, also known as "The Nightwatchman", performed at a convention event and elected as an honorary member

THE Nation.
The Progressive Honor Roll of 2011
MOST VALUABLE MUSICIAN: Tom Morello

2012 REED AWARD
Tom Morello's Union Town Video Campaign

CENTER FOR THE STUDY OF POLITICAL GRAPHICS
THE CULTURE OF LIBERATION AWARD
Honoring Tom Morello

Harry Belafonte presents Hillman Award to Tom Morello for his public service and unrelenting commitment to workers and social justice

Tom Morello to Receive 'Ethical Culture Warrior Award' at Labor 411's Blue Tie Gala

Tom Morello Honoured At WhyHunger Chapin Awards

TOM MORELLO to receive Eleanor Roosevelt Award for Human Rights

Tom Morello to receive MTV prize for historic Occupy Wall Street performance

Tom Morello ROCKS Day One of Convention
Hoffa Presents Tom Morello With Teamsters President's Award

The Nightwatchman

Anti-Walmart protest, Los Angeles. June 30, 2012

I love rock 'n' roll music, but I've also always had one foot squarely in the world of activism.

This was in the midst of a Teamsters strike at Terminal Island in Los Angeles. They called up and said, "Can you come down and play?" I was there later that afternoon.

Teamsters strike, Los Angeles. July 9, 2014

Guess protest, Los Angeles. December, 1997

My mom was very much opposed to both of the Iraq wars so it's hard to say which Bush she's suggesting we dump here, but they both were deserving of the bin.

I've long been a supporter of unions and labor rights and have often participated in civil disobedience actions on their behalf, which has led to a number of stints in jail.

I took part in a protest against the Guess corporation, which was employing sweatshop labor. We blocked the entryway to a store in Santa Monica that sold Guess products and all got carted off to jail.

Iraq War protest

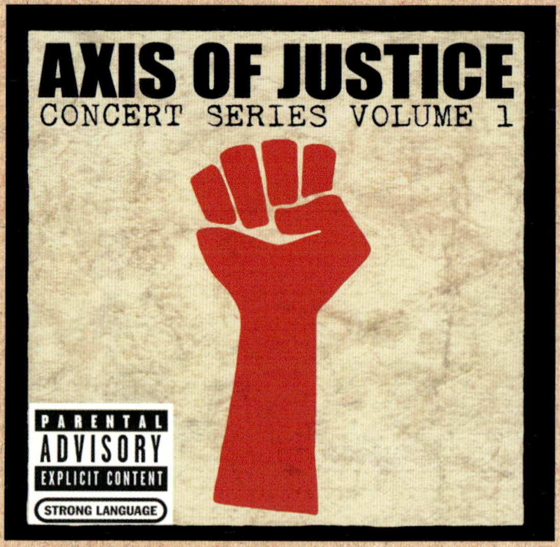

When it became clear to me that Audioslave was not going to be directly involved in political activism, I formed Axis of Justice with Serj Tankian, lead singer of System of a Down, in 2002.

It was a way for fans of our music across the world to connect with local grassroots organizations. It all started when I went to the Ozzfest show in San Bernardino in 2002 and I saw a lot of people with White Power tattoos. Ironically, each of the metal bands on stage that day had at least one non-white member. I thought it was a strange paradox, and that there should be a countervailing anti-racist voice at shows like this.

The question many fans have had through the years is: how do I get involved? Axis of Justice endeavored to provide an answer.

Rally against anti-union bill, Wisconsin State Capitol, Madison, WI. February 21, 2011

There's never been a successful social movement in the United States without a compelling soundtrack. I've always strived to lend my time and my songs to the fight for a more just and decent planet. In turn, those struggles have provided tremendous inspiration through the years.

The global Occupy movement highlighted the grotesque economic inequality and injustice to be found throughout the world. I performed at Occupy encampments in over a dozen countries. There was no PA, no microphones, just people's voices and people's songs.

I could often be found in the streets with my "Black Spartacus" guitar. Mick Jones of the Clash famously called his guitar a heart attack machine, and this became the inspiration for my first love song, "Black Spartacus Heart Attack Machine," which is an ode to this guitar.

Occupy Wall Street, NYC. October 13, 2011

Occupy Wall Street was very inspiring. It really felt like a turning point in the discussion of inequality and injustice in this country.

At the height of the Occupy movement when there were approximately 1,200 Occupy encampments around the globe, I would finish my show in a city and then that night we'd find the local Occupy encampment and play some songs around the fire to express our international solidarity.

As Woody Guthrie famously said, "Take it easy, but take it."

Occupy Wall Street, NYC. October 13, 2011

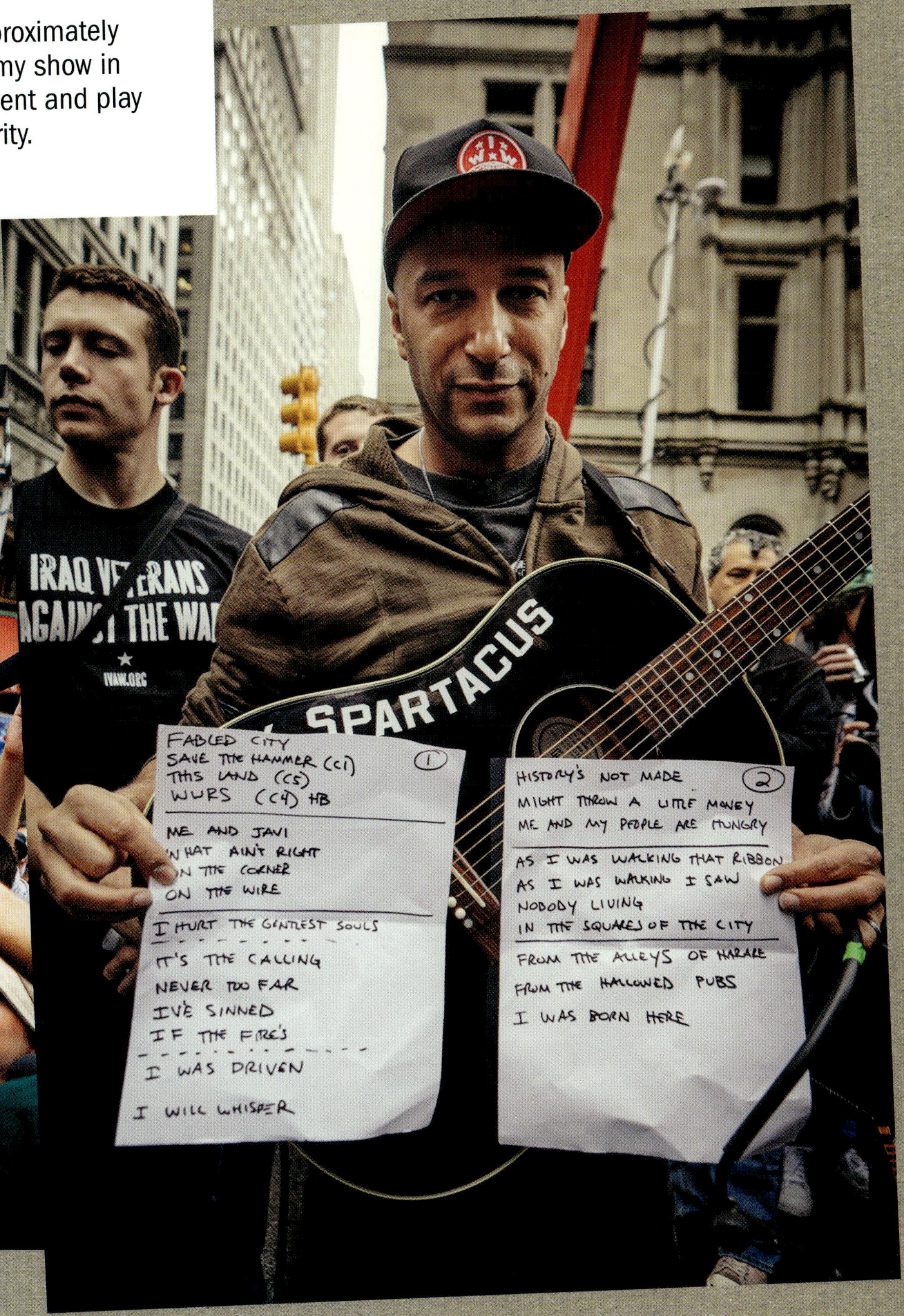

Mary Morello at Occupy LA

Occupy Wall Street one year anniversary, NYC. September 16, 2012

Visiting the memorial of Martin Luther King Jr. 2018

In 1976 over 200 students were massacred by apartheid-enforcing police right here in Soweto, South Africa for raising their fists and singing the African anthem "Morena Boloka Sechaba Sa Heso." On this day, in the same spot, the Morellos sang that same song in their memory.

While I was at Harvard, we built a shantytown in Harvard Yard to protest the university's business dealings with the apartheid. Here I am, revisiting the scene of the crime in 2017 with John Harvard.

Standing with UNITE garment workers in Los Angeles

Rock and Roll Hall of Fame inductions

The reason I was inspired to play a Telecaster was because of the Tele wielded by the great Joe Strummer.

Joe Strummer was my greatest inspiration and my favorite singer of all time and my hero.

I'm grateful to have the tremendous legacy of music that the Clash left behind because through it Joe Strummer and the Clash will continue to inspire and agitate well into the future. In fact, the Clash aren't really gone at all. Because whenever a band cares more about its fans than its bank account, the spirit of the Clash is there. Whenever a band plays as if every single person's soul in the room is at stake, the spirit of the Clash is there. And whenever a stadium band or little garage band has the guts to put their beliefs on the line to make a difference, the spirit of the Clash is there. And whenever people take to the streets to stop an unjust war, the spirit of the Clash is definitely there.

From Tom's speech inducting the Clash into the Rock and Roll Hall of Fame, 2003

I had a strong political streak in me, but I couldn't see how to link that to the music I loved until I discovered the Clash.

London Calling was the record that really showed me that you didn't just have to sing about groupies and the devil; you could also sing about police brutality or the Spanish Civil War, and still make totally compelling music.

Recording "It's a Rockin World" with Joe Strummer and his guitar for the *South Park* soundtrack

Growing up, Kiss was my favorite band—and it wasn't easy being a Kiss fan. Just as Kiss were relentlessly persecuted by critics, their fans were relentlessly persecuted by the self-appointed arbiters of taste in middle schools and high schools across America. Arguments and even fistfights were not uncommon. I recall as a 15-year-old telling one bully, "You can kiss my Kiss-loving ass!" Because Kiss was never a critics' band, Kiss was a people's band.

While there is often a debate about who should and shouldn't be in the Rock and Roll Hall of Fame, I think the criteria are actually quite simple: impact, influence, and awesomeness. Kiss have all three in spades.

From Tom's speech inducting Kiss into the Rock and Roll Hall of Fame, 2014

I came late to folk music. I'd always been a fan of heavy music and it was only when I discovered the first Dylan records and Springsteen's *Nebraska*, and dug back to Woody Guthrie, Phil Ochs, and Joe Hill, that I realized a powerful couplet sung over an acoustic guitar could be as heavy as anything heavy metal has ever created.

One Man Revolution shoot, 2007

"Whatever It Takes" Galvador Ibanez

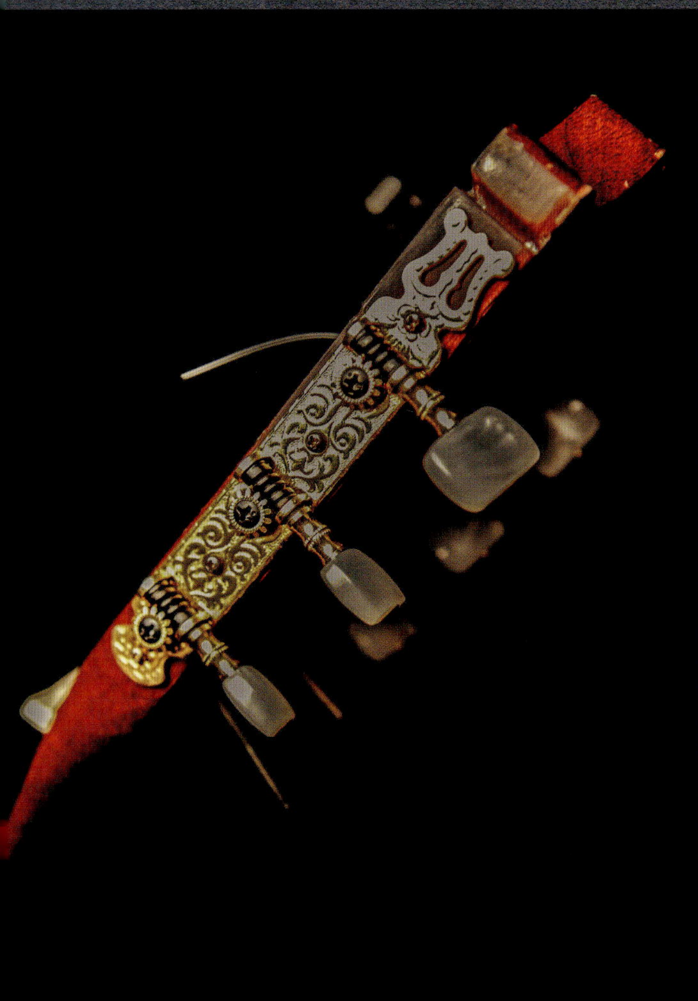

I've always written on a nylon-string acoustic guitar. Big riffs, huge grooves, and plaintive folk ballads all got their start with this guitar. It was the guitar I had around the apartment so I wouldn't terrorize the neighbors with my electric shredding.

One evening I went to a Thanksgiving event at Covenant House, a teen homeless shelter in Hollywood. This kid got up on stage. He was out of tune and his voice shook, but he sang as if everyone's soul in the room was at stake.

That's when I started playing open mic nights around town. My artistic well was not being fully tapped by playing guitar solos and riffs. When I was on an arena tour with Audioslave I'd go to coffee houses on nights off and sign up using my Nightwatchman pseudonym. The latte machine would be whirring in the background as I played my three songs with the same kind of conviction as that kid at Covenant House. It was an artistic reinvention and renewal of enormous proportions for me. I built up a catalog of more than a hundred songs and felt like I'd really found who I was as an artist.

WHATEVER
IT
TAKES

In 2007 I played an acoustic show with Incubus for Amnesty International. Incubus were making a record with Brendan O'Brien at the time and they told him about my solo work. So I sent Brendan some stuff and, to my surprise, he said, "Let's record it." I went to Atlanta and Brendan and I made *One Man Revolution*.

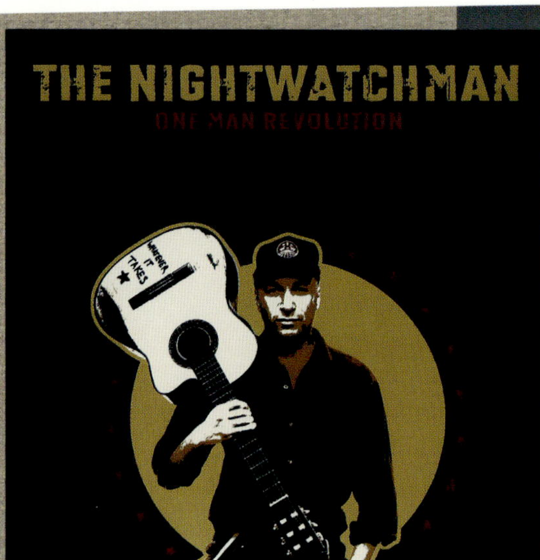

"The Road I Must Travel" music video

The crazy thing is that playing in front of 20,000 people with Audioslave was not a problem. But at the beginning, playing in front of 20 people at an open mic night was nerve-racking until I found my footing.

SXSW, Austin, TX. June 2008

I toured with a missionary zeal. I was back in the van and playing in front of a couple of hundred people a night but I was freed from the trappings of a big band and I could go anywhere, anytime, wherever duty called. When there were anarchists who required bail money in Berkeley, California, I was there.

I remember this one G8 protest in Hamburg, Germany. We had to sneak in on a boat through a military blockade in the harbor and scale a wall. I was the only US artist involved and there was a pitched battle between the police and the Black Bloc activists. As the tear gas was flying, I played my songs and then at nightfall, escaped through the blockade.

I thought, this is what I was born to do.

Stronghold, Venice, CA. April 26, 2010

Each night you try to create a little bit of the world you'd like to see one day.

The Justice Tour, which I set up in 2008 to celebrate the 60th anniversary of the Universal Declaration of Human Rights, was a great vehicle for me to play as the Nightwatchman with a wide range of musicians, some of whom took me outside of my safety zone.

Gilby Clarke, Jerry Cantrell, Carl Restivo, Don Was, Wayne Kramer, myself, Billy Bragg, Steve Van Zandt, Iggy Pop, and Evan Seinfeld (not pictured: Slash and Jakob Dylan) on the Justice Tour stop to benefit Road Recovery, an organization helping young people overcome addiction and abuse.

The whole thing was born out of a residency that I was doing at the Hotel Café in Hollywood. The goal was to create a model of touring that seamlessly integrated charity work and activism with the best and most unexpected show you'd ever seen.

Playing with Ben Harper, Justice Tour

Playing at Sing Sing Prison

Backstage trying to figure out what the hell we were going to play that night

Justice Tour. April 22, 2008

Proceeds from our shows would go to a local charity or activist organization based in the city we were playing. Then on days off the artists on the tour would interact with those organizations.

May Day Rally, Justice Tour, Chicago. May 1, 2008

Honda Center, Anaheim. 2008

The first time I played with Bruce Springsteen was in Anaheim, California in 2008, when he invited me to guest on "The Ghost of Tom Joad." We played the song and it was an electric moment neither of us anticipated.

For the next six years on and off, I was a stage ally of the E Street Band. I couldn't describe it as a dream come true, as I would never have even dared to dream it.

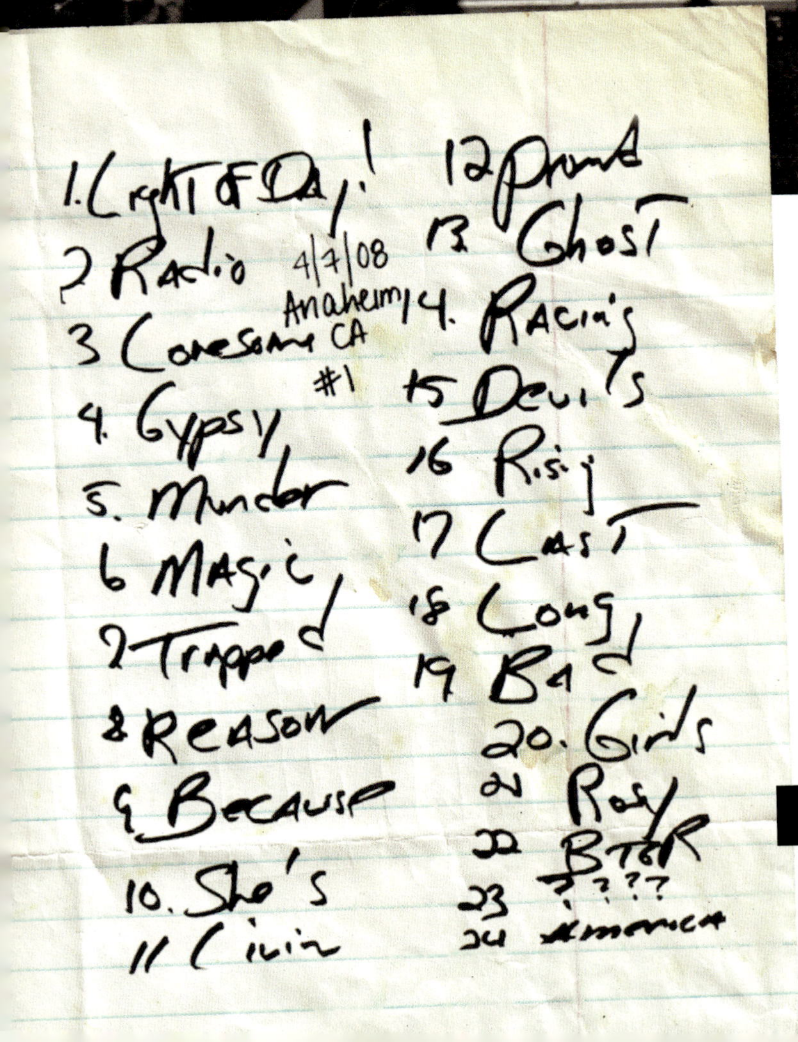

Anaheim setlist

Rehearsing Pete Seeger's 90th birthday celebration
Madison Square Garden, NYC. May 3, 2009

The idea of working with Bruce was so crazy, but after a while I got used to it. And then it would be, "Oh, just me and Bruce back in the dressing room singing a song together"—as we did here at Pete Seeger's 90th birthday party at Madison Square Garden.

One of the most gratifying things that's ever happened in my career was being accepted into the world of the great folk musicians. From Billy Bragg to Steve Earle, these are some of the people I look up to most and it was an honor to play with Pete Seeger a number of times.

My hope was to forge another link in the chain of folk artists who, with three chords and the truth, have endeavored to reshape the world.

Billy Bragg, Steve Earle, and myself singing songs for the people

I'm drawn to the idea that you can use your talent and will to throw your lot in with people who are struggling against injustice. Music can steel the backbone of people who are in these struggles when they realize that they're not alone.

One of the unions I belong to is the Industrial Workers of the World. More than a century ago they compiled the *Little Red Songbook*, which contained all the labor songs of the day, so I appropriated that title for a book containing all the Nightwatchman songs.

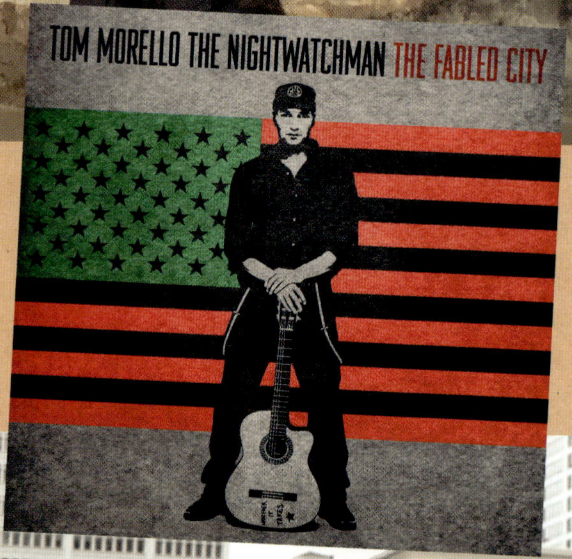

I made the second Nightwatchman record, *The Fabled City*, with Brendan O'Brien. It included additional instrumentation and even a flamenco guitar solo. The album explores themes of loss, ennui, and cosmological dread.

I wrote the *Union Town* EP after a dramatic series of concerts during the union uprising in Madison, Wisconsin, in 2011.

02 Academy, Bristol, UK. November 12, 2011

Frostbite and Freedom: Tom Morello on the Battle of Madison

After a few spirited hours, I was certain: these people in Wisconsin are not going to give up, they are not going to give in and if there is any justice in this world these good people will defeat Governor Walker's awful anti-union bill. This right-wing governor has tried to take advantage of a recession brought on by Wall Street malfeasance to try to ram through legislation that would roll back decades of social progress. But he and his corporate shot callers miscalculated by taking on THESE people. We didn't ask for this fight; Governor Walker tapped us on the shoulder and said, "Let's fight." Okay, dude, it's on. And now we're going to knock your legislative teeth out.

"Union Town" music video

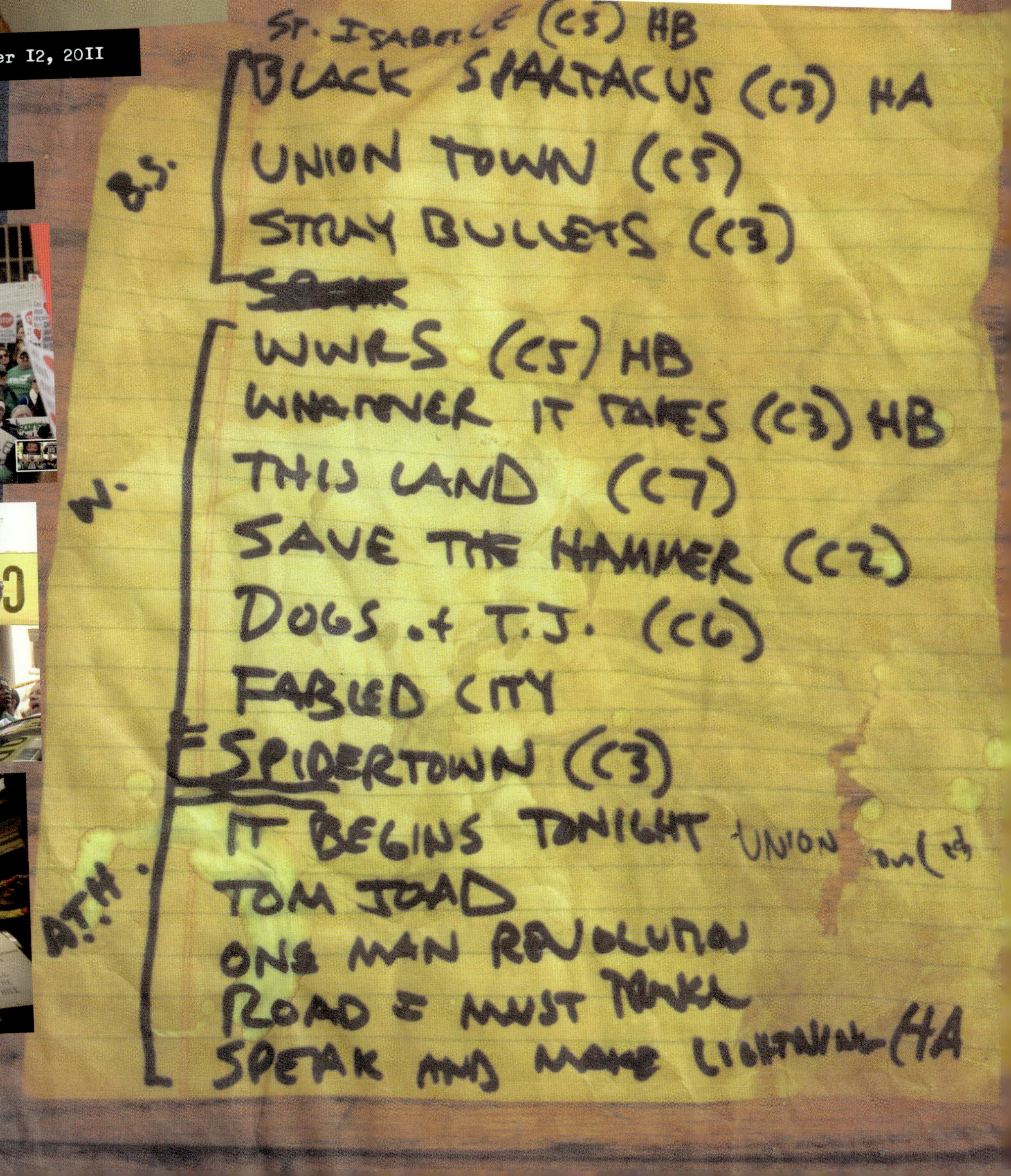

ST. ISABELLE (C3) HB
B.S.
BLACK SPARTACUS (C3) HA
UNION TOWN (C5)
STRAY BULLETS (C3)
N.
WWRS (C5) HB
WHATEVER IT TAKES (C3) HB
THIS LAND (C7)
SAVE THE HAMMER (C2)
DOGS of T.J. (C6)
FABLED CITY
SPIDERTOWN (C3)
A.T.H.
IT BEGINS TONIGHT UNION TOWN (C5)
TOM JOAD
ONE MAN REVOLUTION
ROAD I MUST TRAVEL
SPEAK AND MAKE LIGHTNING HA

Review: 'World Wide Rebel Songs,' Tom Morello/The Nightwatchmen

This kind of high-noon music is rarely made anymore, but in a stunning half-spoken voice that recalls Leonard Cohen and Jakob Dylan, Morello delivers a moving, haunting call to arms worthy of the lineage of Woody Guthrie, Pete Seeger, Bob Dylan and the Clash at those giants' scathing best.

Not for the VMA crowd.

The *World Wide Rebel Songs* album features the Freedom Fighter Orchestra as my backup band. In the live performances, we ramped up the electric elements with shredding solos to go along with the acoustic material.

Opening for Bruce Springsteen
Hard Rock Calling, Hyde Park, London. July 14, 2012

I performed on the streets and in the backyards at the SXSW music festival.

Singing "This Land Is Your Land"

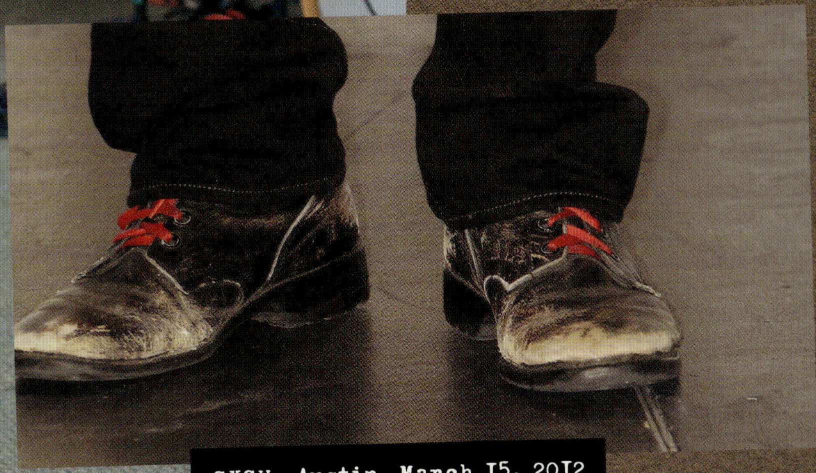

SXSW, Austin. March 15, 2012

These are the same shoes I wore for the first Rage Against the Machine club show in 1991.

My belief is that the essence of solo performance is usually pretty clear right off the bat: you've either got it or you don't.

Outside Lands Music and Arts Festival, San Francisco. August 12, 2012

I played a show at the very prestigious and fancy Lincoln Center in New York City. I think they got more than they bargained for when I invited the entire crowd up on stage for the finale. From my beginnings up in Harlem at 142nd and Riverside to headlining a show at the Lincoln Center was not a journey I would have ever predicted.

Allen Room, Lincoln Center, New York City. February 16, 2013

Allen Room, Lincoln Center, New York City. February 16, 2013

Wrecking Ball tour, Los Angeles Arena, Los Angeles. April 2012

Bruce Springsteen asked me to join the E Street Band for an Australian run when guitarist Steve Van Zandt was away filming his TV series *Lilyhammer*. I stayed on for the next few years touring with Bruce.

The only person I would ever be a sideman for is Bruce. 'Cause believe me, I am not a casual Springsteen fan. He's the only friend I have who I subscribe to a fanzine about.

Part of what makes Bruce's shows great is that no one in the band or the audience knows what the next song is going to be. I familiarized myself with about 250 songs before the tour began and there were many more to learn along the way. During my last US tour with the band, we played 193 different songs in 34 shows.

It was an honor to be asked to play on a number of tracks for Springsteen's *Wrecking Ball* album. The solo on "Jack of All Trades" is one of my favorites.

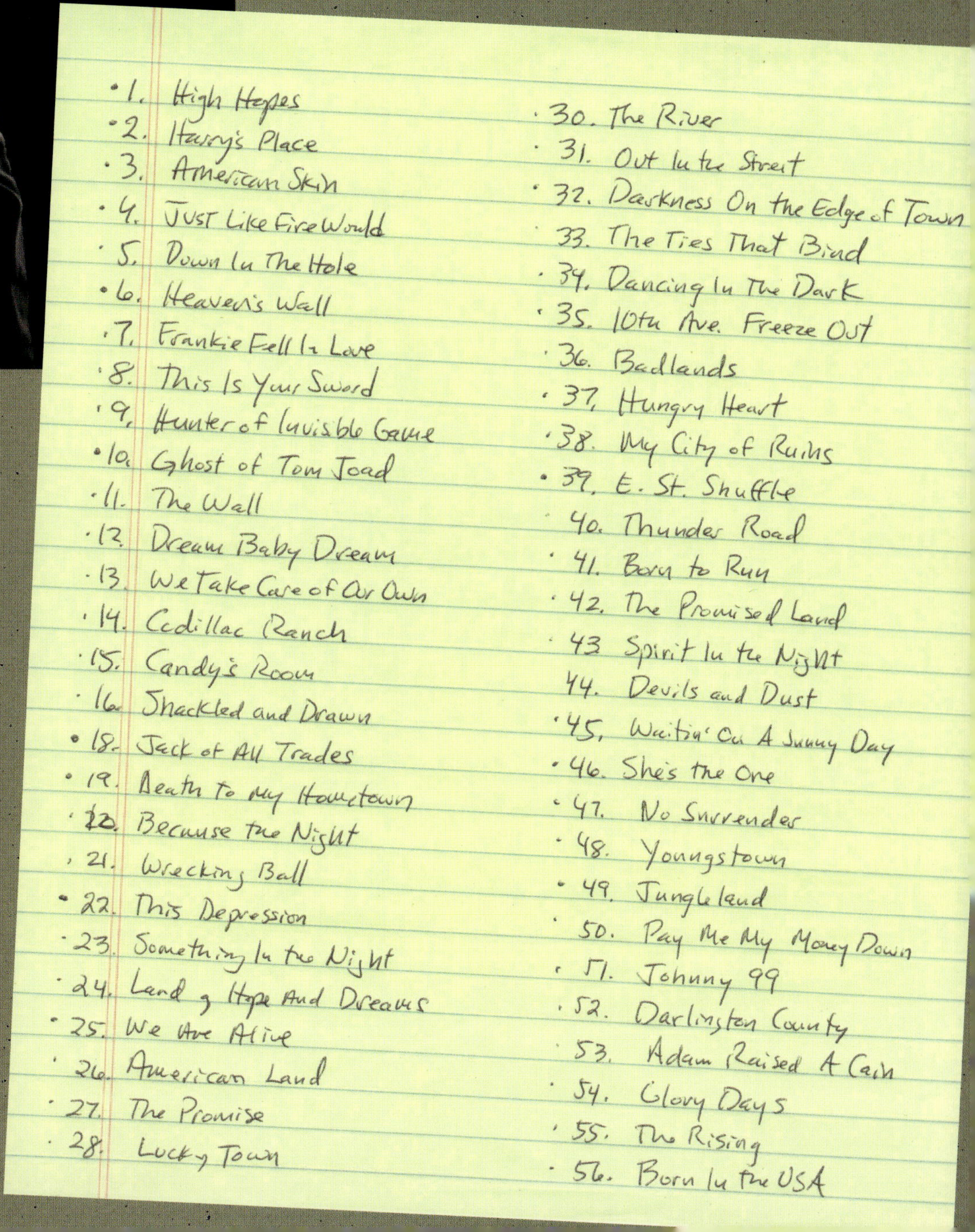

1. High Hopes
2. Harry's Place
3. American Skin
4. Just Like Fire Would
5. Down In The Hole
6. Heaven's Wall
7. Frankie Fell In Love
8. This Is Your Sword
9. Hunter of Invisible Game
10. Ghost of Tom Joad
11. The Wall
12. Dream Baby Dream
13. We Take Care of Our Own
14. Cadillac Ranch
15. Candy's Room
16. Shackled and Drawn
18. Jack of All Trades
19. Death to My Hometown
20. Because the Night
21. Wrecking Ball
22. This Depression
23. Something In the Night
24. Land of Hope And Dreams
25. We Are Alive
26. American Land
27. The Promise
28. Lucky Town
30. The River
31. Out In the Street
32. Darkness On the Edge of Town
33. The Ties That Bind
34. Dancing In The Dark
35. 10th Ave. Freeze Out
36. Badlands
37. Hungry Heart
38. My City of Ruins
39. E. St. Shuffle
40. Thunder Road
41. Born to Run
42. The Promised Land
43. Spirit In the Night
44. Devils and Dust
45. Waitin' On A Sunny Day
46. She's the One
47. No Surrender
48. Youngstown
49. Jungleland
50. Pay Me My Money Down
51. Johnny 99
52. Darlington County
53. Adam Raised A Cain
54. Glory Days
55. The Rising
56. Born In the USA

While on tour in Australia in 2013 the E Street Band began recording songs that would appear on the *High Hopes* album. Bruce seemed very inspired by what was going on onstage and wanted to bring it into the studio.

Recording *High Hopes*, Studios 301, Sydney, Australia

High Hopes tour, Tampa, Florida. April, 2014

In his late sixties he was playing four-hour shows and crowd-surfing. Bruce gives every ounce of himself every night.

Here's the thing about Bruce. People travel all over the world to see his shows. Those people are very excited to be in the room to see Bruce Springsteen. But no one is more excited to be there than Bruce himself. Every night he'd say, "I've played shows for 45 years, but tonight's going to be the best one."

Mohegan Sun Arena, Uncasville, CT. May 17, 2014

On the last night of the High Hopes tour, in Connecticut, of the first seven songs we did, six of them we were playing for the first time on the tour. The other song, which we had played only once before, was "Jump" by Van Halen. You really had to keep on your toes.

Cynthia Woods Mitchell Pavilion, The Woodlands, TX. May 6, 2014

HIGH HOPES (whammy: octave down)

Vamp
| Am | Am | Am | Am |

Verse 1
| Am | Am | Am | Am |
| Am | Am | Am | Am |

Pre
| G | G | Am | Am |
| G | G | C | E7 | E7 |

Chorus
| Am C | G Am | Am C | G Am |
| Am C | G Am | Am C | G Am |

Verse 2
| Am | Am | Am | Am |
| Am | Am | Am | Am |

Pre
| G | G | Am | Am |
| G | G | C | E7 | E7 |

Chorus

HUNTER OF INVISIBLE GAME

Capo 4

Verse 1 & 2 & Vamp
| C | Csus4 | G7 | C |

Chorus
Am	F	G7	C
Am	F	G	C
Am	F	G7	C
Am	G	F	C

Vamp
| C | Csus4 | G | C |
| C | Csus4 | G | C |

Verse 3
| C | Csus4 | G7 | C |

Vamp
| C | Csus4 | G | C |

Chorus
Am	F	G7	C
Am	F	G	C
Am	F	G7	C
Am	G	F	C

AMERICAN SKIN (whammy: oct down)

Intro
| A | A | F#m | F#m | E | E | Dmaj7 | D |

Verse 1
| A | A | F#m | F#m | E | E | Dmaj7 | D |
| A | A | F#m | F#m | E | E | Dmaj7 | D |

Pre
| D | A/C# | D | A/C# |

Chorus
D A/C# Bm	D A/C# Bm
D A/C# Bm	D A/C# Bm
D A/C# Bm	D A/C# Bm	E

Verse 2
| A | A | F#m | F#m | E | E | Dmaj7 | D |
| A | A | F#m | F#m | E | E | Dmaj7 | D |

Pre
| D | A/C# | D | A/C# |

Chorus
D A/C# Bm	D A/C# Bm
D A/C# Bm	D A/C# Bm
D A/C# Bm	D A/C# Bm	E

Re-Intro
| A | A | F#m | F#m | E | E | Dmaj7 | D |

At the Imagine: John Lennon 75th Birthday Concert I got to play "Working Class Hero" with Kris Kristofferson and some other luminaries. I also had the chance to play a shredding solo during "Power to the People."

John Lennon's 75th Birthday Concert
Madison Square Garden, New York City. December 5, 2015

MetLife Stadium, East Rutherford, NJ. August 25, 2016

At four hours and one minute, the show at the MetLife Stadium was the longest Bruce Springsteen had ever played in the US.

"The Ghost of Tom Joad" is the song that started it all. It was in the set every night, and always blew the roof off the place.

Asbury Park, NJ

POR
Unfuck the World
Testify
Take the Power Back
Living on the 110
Hail to the Chief
Guerrilla Radio
Legalize Me
Fight the Power

Hand on the Pump
Can't Truss It
Insane - N - Brain
Bring the Noise
Aint Going Out
Terrordome
Jump Around

Sleep Now Fire (Cochise) ← PULL BACKDROP
Like a Stone
Radical Eyes
Know Your Enemy
Strength in Numbers
Bullet in the Head
How I could just Kill a Man
Bulls On Parade
Killing

9/9/17

Prophets of Rage

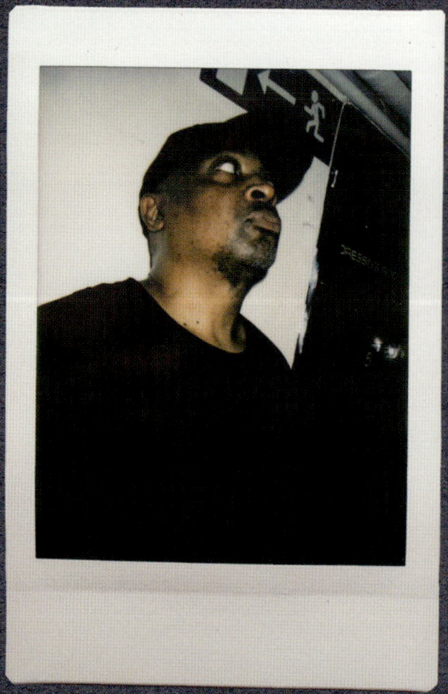

In 2016 American politics was in chaos. I figured we had to do more than tweet about it, so I called up some friends—Tim and Brad, and Chuck D from Public Enemy. Then DJ Lord, also from Public Enemy, and B-Real from Cypress Hill joined the fold and we came out guns blazing as Prophets of Rage.

There was a headline on CNN: "Donald Trump rages against the machine." We said, "Oh hell no." We've been raging against injustice for decades and aimed to create a soundtrack for the resistance.

Verizon Wireless Amphitheatre, Alpharetta, GA. October 4, 2016

The first ten shows were either free or we gave 100% of the proceeds to a worthy cause. By embracing the catalogs of Rage Against the Machine, Public Enemy, and Cypress Hill, we were the avengers embarking on our own musical Infinity War.

Free Skid Row show, Los Angeles. July 15, 2016

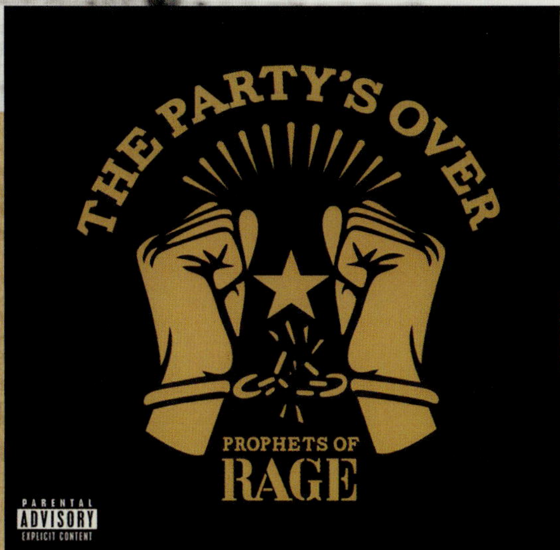

Republican National Convention, Cleveland. July, 2016

Shoreline Amphitheatre, Mountain View, CA. September 13, 2016

Forum, Los Angeles. September 15, 2016

Dave Grohl joined us at the Forum to kick out the jams. It was awesome to return to this historic LA venue with a new band.

Forum, LA. September 20, 2016

Mary Morello with Brendan O'Brien

Mary Morello busting into rehearsal and giving us some suggestions

A famous person of Irish descent and Bono

My mom taught high school for over 30 years and I occasionally hear from her former students. Many say she was the most important educator in their lives and pushed them beyond their limits and made sure they saw far beyond the borders of our conservative homogenous suburb. She helped them learn to care and advocate for people less fortunate, people oppressed by race and color lines from Cabrini Green in Chicago to the fields of California and Cesar Chavez. And she did it all with humor and acceptance inspiring generations of students. One fan said after my mom introduced the band with her standard, "Please welcome THE BEST FUCKING BAND IN THE UNIVERSE!!" intro, "She was so fucking cool and it made me proud to start circling that pit as she walked off the stage to the sounds of wailing sirens. She was like a general signaling the start of a war."

Chris Cornell and I played a show in Seattle at a tiny club called El Corazón. Under its former name, the Off Ramp, it's the place where grunge was born. We were campaigning for the minimum wage to be raised to $15. It was a great night.

15 Now benefit, El Corazón, Seattle. September 26, 2014

On the night of Trump's inauguration, Prophets of Rage hosted an Anti-Inaugural Ball. It featured an incredible array of anti-inaugural talent, including Jackson Browne, Vic Mensa, and Tenacious D. We were also joined on stage by a "Freedom Choir" formed of activists from various LA grassroots organizations.

Anti-Inaugural Ball, Los Angeles. January 20, 2017

The highlight, of course, was that it was the night of the first Audioslave performance in 12 years; Chris Cornell joined us on stage for a three-song set of "Cochise," "Like a Stone," and "Show Me How to Live." It was beautiful to stand on stage with our friend for what would be the last time.

Ever since Chris's passing, we've performed an instrumental version of "Like A Stone" with an empty microphone in the spotlight. The audience sings the melody as a communal prayer to celebrate Chris's life and memory.

You're a prince, you're a snare, you're a shadow
You're twilight and star burn and shade
You're a sage, you're a wound shared, you're masked
You're a pillar of smoke, you're a platinum heart
You're a brush fire, you're caged, you're free
Your vision pierces, you do not see
You are pieces strewn on the hillside
You're open armed, you're armed, you're true
You're a revealer of visions, you're the passenger, you're a never-fading scar
You're twilight and star burn and shade
You're the secret veiled, you're the secret revealed, you're surrounded no more
You're not there, now you're always here
You're a handsome groom, a loving father, a haunted stairwell
You're the clear bell ringing, the mountains echo your song
Maybe no one has ever known you
You are twilight and star burn and shade

I wrote this poem the night Chris passed.

Vive Latino, Mexico City. March 18, 2017

Hellfest, Clisson, France. June 18, 2017

Rock Am Ring, Nürburgring, Germany. June 4, 2017

Stretching it out. Got to keep the Achilles limber.

Movistar Arena, Santiago, Chile. May 3, 2017

Los Angeles Times

Tom Morello on why activism in music matters: 'Dangerous times demand dangerous songs'

This election season it feels like we are in Pompeii with the volcano erupting and the only boat out of town is the Titanic. Do I vote? Yes, I do, but casting a ballot into the void every four years for one of the two monopoly party candidates is not enough. The master's tools will never dismantle the master's house.

Movistar Arena, Santiago, Chile. May 3, 2017

The sonics of Cypress Hill and Public Enemy were a huge influence on my guitar playing. Chuck D and B-Real are titans of their craft, generous souls, and lovely humans.

Download Festival, Paris, France. June 11, 2017

As a ritual before each Prophets of Rage show, we'd get our hands in and on the count of three say one word about that particular night. It was always city specific or had something to do with world events of the day.

Hellfest, Clisson, France. June 18, 2017

Here with the sage of hip-hop, Chuck D, most likely talking baseball.

Download Festival, Madrid, Spain. June 24, 2017

Theatre of Living Arts, Philadelphia. September 10, 2017

Download Festival, Paris, France. June 11, 2017

"Hands Up" video shoot. 2017

NOBODY
FOR
PRESIDENT

Zepp, Nagoya, Japan. April 3, 2018

Gröna Lund, Stockholm, Sweden. June 26, 2018

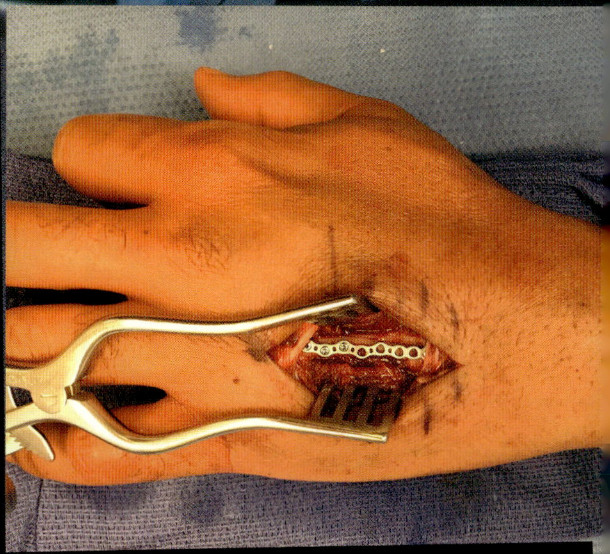

Surgery on fourth metacapal. June 23, 2018

Four days before a Prophets of Rage European tour I shattered my fourth metacarpal. I broke it on a Thursday, flew home Friday, had surgery Saturday, got on a plane Sunday, landed in Sweden on Monday, and on Tuesday played a 90-minute set.

The world is not going to change itself; that is up to you. The people who've changed the world in radical or even revolutionary ways, throughout history, are people who had no more money, courage, power, influence, or creativity than anybody watching or listening to us.

CASHLESS

Tuesday, October 29, 2019

Dallas, TX
House of Blues

OPPORTUNITY COST VIDEO
THE GRAIN ELEVATOR COMMUNIQUE VIDEO
LEAD POISONING
WHERE IT'S AT AIN'T WHAT IT IS
WHAT DOES FREEDOM MEAN TO YOU VIDEO
BATTLE SIRENS
RABBIT'S REVENGE
EVERY STEP THAT I TAKE
HOW LONG
THE LITTLE LAMB COMMUNIQUE VIDEO
OFF BROADWAY / COCHISE / LIKE A STONE
CAN'T STOP THE BLEEDING
POPCORN
FIND ANOTHER WAY
THE MUSIC IS VIOLENT WE ARE NOT VIDEO
HOUSE GONE UP IN FLAMES
SAVE THE HAMMER FOR THE MAN
THE GARDEN OF GETHSEMANE
THE WALLS OF JERICHO COMMUNIQUE VIDEO
VIGILANTE *NOCTURNO*
FAMOUS LAST WORDS VIDEO
GHOST OF TOM JOAD
KILLING IN THE NAME
POWER TO THE PEOPLE

The Atlas Underground

On my 19th studio album, *The Atlas Underground*, I took a bold stab at creating a new genre of music by forging an alloy of Marshall-stack riff rock, crazy guitar sounds, electronic dance music, and dangerous truths. I wanted it to have the potency of kick ass rock 'n' roll combined with a sonic template looking to the future.

My first 18 albums were made with a bunch of guys standing in a room, toe to toe, and eyeball to eyeball, cranking up their amps and giving it their all. I wanted to make an artistic departure and leap with *The Atlas Underground* by making music in a variety of ways that would get me out of my safety zone and lead to greater experimentation.

This photo pays homage to Joe Hill. He was the poet laureate of the US working class in the early 20th century and a member of the Industrial Workers of the World union. He wrote many of the most famous labor anthems of all time, including "Solidarity Forever." He was framed on murder charges and executed by a Utah firing squad in 1915, but it was really his politics and his songs that were his crime. They pinned a heart in crosshairs to his chest so the firing squad wouldn't miss. We appropriated that symbol for *The Atlas Underground* as we were aiming for the heart as well.

Here I am with Freedom Fighter Orchestra stalwarts Carl Restivo (left) and Eric Gardner (right). (The other member, Dave Gibbs, is not pictured.) They are tremendous musicians and loyal companions who have rocked hundreds of shows with me around the world. Carl, for years, has been my musical consigliere, recording albums, transcribing Springsteen songs, and is an invaluable sounding board in my musical life.

With the winged hippopotamus album cover, I wanted an image that would capture both the heavy metal gravitas and the surreal digital beauty we were aiming for.

Samsung Best of Blues Festival, Sao Paulo, Brazil. September 16, 2018

The notion from the very start was to forge this sonic conspiracy of like-minded artists from wide-ranging genres, and then curate it into a powerful and cohesive whole.

Performing "Every Step That I Take" with Portugal. The Man and Whethan on *Jimmy Kimmel Live!* October 10, 2018

Atlas Underground collaborators

From top left: Tom Morello, Marcus Mumford, Knife Party, Portugal. The Man, Bassnectar, Killer Mike, Vic Mensa, Herobust, Whethan, K.Flay, GZA, RZA, Big Boi, Carl Restivo, Tim McIlrath, Gary Clark Jr., Pretty Lights, Leikeli47, Steve Aoki, Nico Stadi

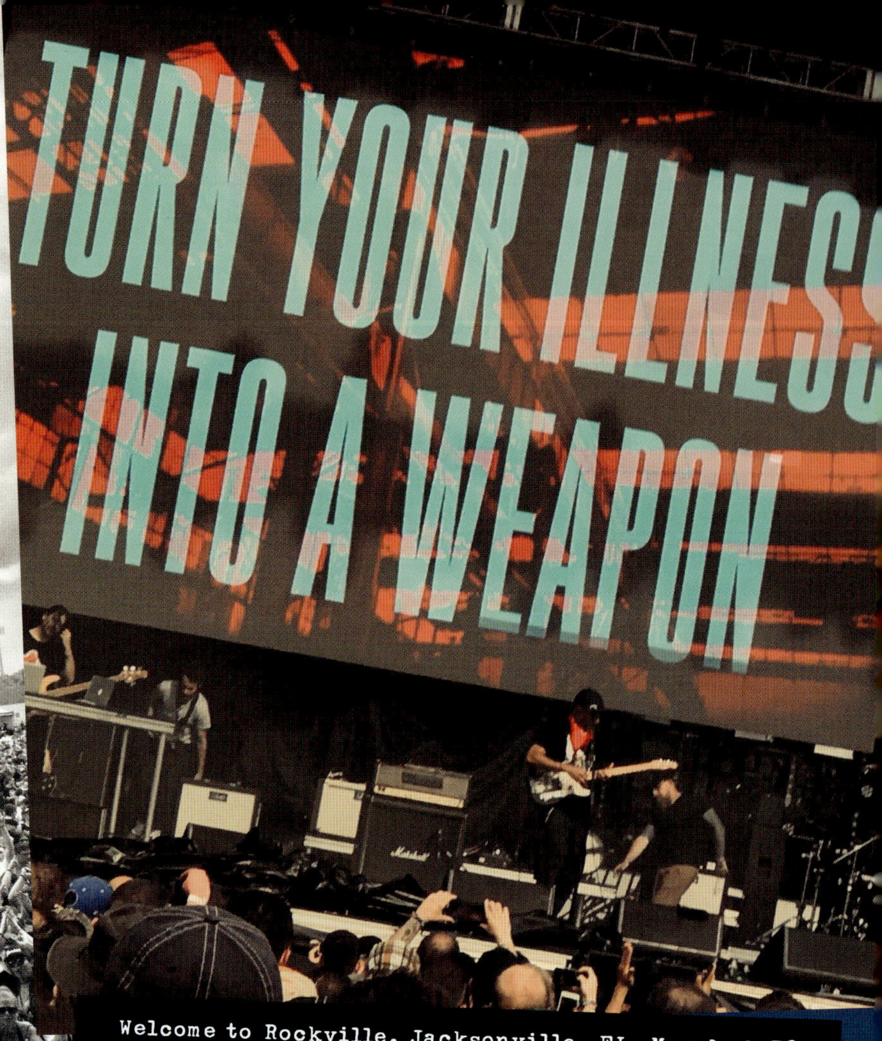

Welcome to Rockville, Jacksonville, FL. May 3, 2019

Jamming with *Atlas Underground* collaborator Marcus Mumford

Brooklyn Bowl, Las Vegas. November 3, 2019

The challenge was turning an album that had 20 collaborators into basically a one-man live show. Sean Evans (the artistic director for Roger Waters's Wall and Us and Them tours) and I came up with an experience that's somewhere between a crazy mosh pit, an illegal rave, a subversive art installation, and a prison riot.

MADIBA
anti-fascist

Welcome to Rockville, Jacksonville, FL. May 3, 2019

On tour with Muse, Manchester, UK. June, 2019

Hard Halloween Red Rocks, Red Rocks Amphitheatre, CO. October 26, 2019

Commodore Ballroom, Vancouver, Canada. November 7, 2019

Brooklyn Bowl, Las Vegas. November 3, 2019

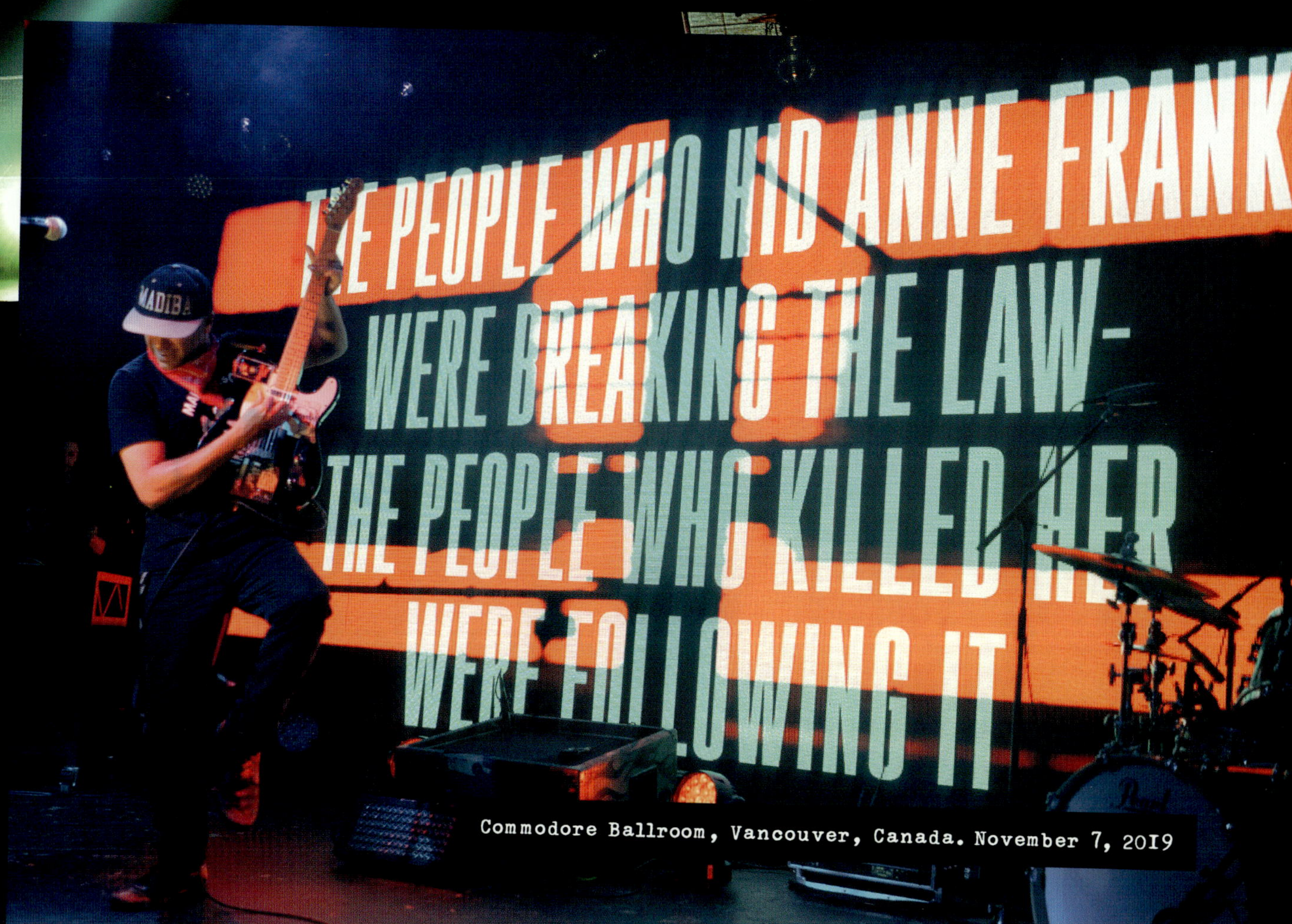

Commodore Ballroom, Vancouver, Canada. November 7, 2019

Varsity Theater, Minneapolis. October 21, 2019

SXSW, Austin, TX. March, 2019

Vic Theatre, Chicago. October 22, 2019

Vic Theatre, Chicago. October 22, 2019

Performing "Save the Hammer for the Man", Los Angeles. 2019

Brooklyn Bowl, Las Vegas. November 3, 2019

When I was approached by the Metropolitan Museum of Art to have my guitars put alongside those of Jimmy Page, Eddie Van Halen, and Keith Richards, it took me quite a while to get up off the floor.

Guitar World photo shoot, Los Angeles. 2014

I've always felt that my guitar playing is more of a mission than a career. It's a constant tug of war. I'm both blessed and cursed to be a guitar player. I didn't choose it, it chose me. Then the challenge is to find a way to weave my convictions into my music in a meaningful way.

My mission has had many incarnations, but the North Star that continues to guide my journey is that I've got six strings and a couple of unapologetic ideas to share. I'm not sure that a guitar can be used as a sledgehammer of justice, but I aim to find out.

The publishers would like to thank:
Tom Morello, for sharing his convictions, commitment, and wit in the course of making this book.

Thank you to everyone at Vector Management:
Ken Levitan, Nicki Loranger, Erin Hanson, George Muench

Thank you to Chuck D, Nora Guthrie, Michael Moore and Jann Wenner for their introductions to the book.

The Genesis team:
Uchenna Achebe, Francesca Balgobind, Katy Baker, James Hodgson, Bruce Hopkins, Stephanie Luff, Sally Millard, Nicky Page, Alexandra Rigby-Wild, Marguerite Rooke, Rosie Strandberg and James Tribe

Thanks to my mom, Mary Morello, for her warrior DNA and for her lifelong unconditional love and support… and for letting me practice in her basement then, and now. Thanks to my kids, Rhoads, Roman and Ruby for making it obvious that the future is worth fighting for. Thanks to everyone at Genesis Publications and Erin Hanson, Nicki Loranger, and Ken Levitan at Vector Management for their patience and tireless support in putting this book together. Thanks to all the photographers whose deft eyes capture art and activism as it unfolds. A mighty thanks to all my band mates and musical collaborators through the years, principally of course Zack, Tim, and Brad without whom you likely would have little interest in this book. And the greatest thanks to my lovely wife, Denise, for her love, insightful editorial wisdom, and for being the only member of our family who knows how to use the scanner.

REBEL

Gallery

GOD
HATES
FLAGS

CLASS WAR
JUST DO IT

rage against
the machine
rage against
the machine

NEWS

World Domination
Goes better with Coke
ORCHID
DARK HORSE COMICS
3
$3.50
TOM MORELLO
SCOTT HEPBURN
DAN JACKSON
ЛЕНИН
TOM YOU'RE
MY REASON TO
PLAY GUITAR!!!

rage
singer
prophets
activist
MAKE AMERICA RAGE AGAIN
VICTOR JARA LIVES
UNITE
SOUL POWER
43
BROKEN FINGERS
THE ATLAS UNDERGROUND
TOM MORELLO
Tom Morello
ARM THE HOMELESS
SCRATCH! SCRATCH!

Sidekick Bass 50
Fender
FUCK TRUMP
ARM THE HOMELESS
RESERVED FOR
TOM FUCKEN MORELLO
UNITE
FEED THE POOR
FIGHT THE POWER
ROCK THE F**K OUT
Tom Morello
Whammy
ARM THE HOMELESS
POWER
BRAZIL AGAINST THE FASCISM
Prophets Of Rage
そだねー
Tom Morello
TOM MORELLO
UNITE
SOUL POWER

CREDITS

With special thanks to Lindsay Brice, Danny Clinch, Lisa Johnson, Lisa S Johnson and Eitan Miskevich.

All reasonable effort has been made to identify and contact the copyright holders of the images and artwork in this publication. Any omissions are inadvertent.

PHOTOGRAPHY AND EPHEMERA

Copyright © Alamy
David Atlas / MediaPunch / Alamy
Page 80 (top)
Kevin Estrada / MediaPunch / Alamy
Page 108 (bottom)
Everett Collection / Alamy
Page 201 (top row, second from left)
WENN Rights Ltd / Alamy
Pages 81, 110, 111, 145 (left)

Copyright © Austin American-Statesman
Page 145 (top right)

Copyright © Gavin Batty
Page 187 (top)

Copyright © Lindsay Brice
Pages 36 (top), 40 (top left), 42 (top and center), 43 (right), 45, 48, 49

Copyright © Nick Caito
Page 152

Copyright © Brett Callwood
Page 179 (top left cover photo)

Copyright © Brett Carpenter / LA Weekly
Pages 184 (left), 190 (top row and bottom left) 192, 200 (top row, third from left)

Copyright © Greg Chow
Page 180

Copyright © Danny Clinch
Pages 129 (top and right), 134 (top), 141 (top right), 147 (top), 148, 155 (top)

Copyright © Philip Cosores
Page 163 (top)

Copyright © Chuck D
Page 9

Copyright © Liz Dueling / Revenant Media
Page 186 (top right)

Copyright © Alejandro Ernesto / EPA / Shutterstock
Page 106 (bottom)

Copyright © Sandlin Gaither
Page 139 (top left)

Copyright © Getty Images
Mark Baker / Getty Images
Page 50
Paul Bergen / Redferns / Getty Images
Pages 100 (bottom), 101, 108 (top left)
Lindsay Brice / Getty Images
Pages 38, 39, 40 (top right), 44, 46, 52, 55 (top right, bottom left), 68 (bottom)
Andrew Burton / Getty Images
Page 130 (bottom)
Michael Campanella / Redferns / Getty Images
Page 175 (bottom left)
Manuel Lagos Cid / Paris Match / Getty Images
Page 169
L Cohen / Getty Images
Page 99
Nigel Crane / Redferns / Getty Images
Page 104
Paul R Giunta / Getty Images
Page 158 (bottom)
Christie Goodwin / Getty Images
Pages 86 (bottom), 87 (bottom), 88 (top right)
Jesse Grant / WireImage / Getty Images
Page 109
Dan Griffiths / Photoshot / Getty Images
Page 136 (right)
Jo Hale / Getty Images
Page 82 (bottom)
Frazer Harrison / Getty Images
Page 200 (bottom center)
Rune Hellestad / Corbis / Getty Images
Page 144 (left)
Randy Holmes / Getty Images
Page 184 (right)
Hiroyuki Ito / Getty Images
Page 147 (bottom)
Gie Knaeps / Getty Images
Pages 53 (right), 65
Joe Kohen / WireImage / Getty Images
Page 138 (top right)
Jeff Kravitz / Getty Images
Pages 62, 160 (bottom)
Scott Legato / FilmMagic / Getty Images
Page 118
Michael Loccisano / Getty Images
Page 138 (top left)
Stephen Lovekin / Getty Images
Page 141 (bottom)
Kevin Mazur / WireImage / Getty Images
Pages 98 (top), 108 (top right), 112, 113, 141 (top left)
Catherine McGann / Getty Images
Page 43 (left)
Ethan Miller / Getty Images
Page 79
Gary Miller / Getty Images
Page 153
Tim Mosenfelder / Getty Images
Pages 64, 80 (bottom), 160 (top), endpapers (hippo image)
NBC / Getty Images
Page 67
Doug Pesinger / Getty Images
Page 83 (top)
Suzi Pratt / FilmMagic / Getty Images
Page 162
Joby Sessions / Total Guitar Magazine / Getty Images
Page 143 (top left)
John Shearer / WireImage / Getty Images
Page 103
Andy Sheppard / Getty Images
Page 87 (top right)
Ted Soqui / Corbis / Getty Images
Page 124 (top)
Jim Spellman / WireImage / Getty Images
Pages 132 (top), 145 (bottom right)
Mark Sullivan / Wire Image / Getty Images
Page 142 (top left)
Greetsia Tent / Getty Images
Page 82 (top)
Eric Thayer / Getty Images
Page 87 (top left)
Sean tSabhasaigh / WireImage / Getty Images
Page 163 (bottom)
Scott Varley / MediaNews Group / Orange County Register / Getty Images
Page 124 (bottom right)
Noel Vasquez / Getty Images
Page 89
Theo Wargo / Getty Images
Pages 98 (bottom), 154, endpapers ("end racism", "imagine", "if not for you" signs)
Jim Watson / AFP / Getty Images
Page 159 (bottom)
Kevin Winter / Getty Images
Pages 84 (bottom left) 119, 159 (top), 199, endpapers ("not my president" sign)

Copyright © Stephen Green
Page 16 (bottom right)

Copyright © Carol Gronner
Pages 137, 138 (center), 139 (bottom), 161 (top right)

Copyright © Ismael Guerra
Page 186 (top left)

Copyright © Piero F Gunti
Page 123 (bottom right)

Copyright © Oliver Halfin
Page 11

Copyright © Ross Halfin
Page 196 (bottom)

Copyright © Erin Hanson
Page 131 (top left)

Copyright © Jon Hermison
Page 195 (top)

Copyright © Lisa Johnson Rock Photographer
Pages 35, 47 (bottom), 56, 57, 66

Copyright © Lisa S Johnson
Pages 51, 60 (right), 61 (top), 74, 75, 94 (top and bottom), 134 (left), 135

Copyright © Bruce Kessler / RockinHouston.com
Page 69 (top)

Copyright © Tracy Ketcher
Page 138 (bottom left)

Copyright © Teemu Korpijaakko
Page 121

Copyright © Sacha Lecca
Page 128

Copyright © Nicole Lemberg
Page 174

Copyright © Jo Lopez
Pages 150, 155 (bottom)

Copyright © Griffin Lotz
Page 129 (bottom left)

Copyright © Lutron Photography
Pages 157 (bottom left), 175 (top left)

Copyright © Narayan Mahon
Page 127

Copyright © Eitan Miskevich
Pages 84 (bottom right), 114 (bottom), 157 (top right and bottom right), 166, 167, 168, 170, 171, 172, 173, 175 (top right), 176, 177

Copyright © Paul Moore
Page 144 (right)

Copyright © Rhoads Morello
Page 124 (bottom left)

Copyright © Fred Morledge / Kabik Photo Group
Pages 187 (bottom), 197

Copyright © Tracy Morter
Page 86 (top)

Copyright © Yuri Murakami
Page 183

Copyright © J Michael Neal
Page 139 (top right)

Copyright © Darrole Palmer
Pages 189 (bottom), 191 (top and bottom)

Copyright © Paramount Pictures
Page 201 (second row, second from left)

Copyright © Levi Pervin / levrock@mac.com
Page 140

Copyright © Joseph Quever
Page 149 (top left)

Copyright © Dustin Rabin
Pages 78, 123 (top right)

Copyright © REUTERS / Mariana Bazo MB / stock.adobe.com
Pages 106 (top), 107

Copyright © Sean Ricigliano
Pages 133, 165

Photo courtesy of the Rock & Roll Hall of Fame, Cleveland, Ohio
Page 196 (top)

Copyright © 2003 Rolling Stone. All rights reserved. Used by permission.
Pages 84 (news item), 143 (news item)

Copyright © San Antonio Express-News / ZUMA Press
Page 144 (top right news item)

Copyright © Rocky Schenck
Pages 28 (center), 29 (top right)

Copyright © Martin Schoeller / AUGUST
Page 70

Copyright © Seth Shapiro / Rockshowpix
Page 193 (top left)

Copyright © Lori Shepler
Page 55 (top left image)

Copyright © Samuel Silkworth / Silky Shots
Page 181 (bottom center)

Copyright © Randal Slavin
Pages 117, 146

Copyright © Socks&iPhone
Page 190 (bottom right)

Copyright © David A Solorzano
Pages 123 (left), 188, 193 (bottom and top right), 194 (top)

Photos courtesy of Sony Music Entertainment
Pages 76, 77, 91, 92, 93, 94 (center), 95, 96, 100 (top left), 114 (top), 115. Photos by Danny Clinch

Copyright © Pamela Springsteen
Page 71 (all photos except bottom right)

Copyright © Tom Stone
Page 130 (top)

Copyright © Romy Suskin
Page 120

Copyright © Phil Thach
Page 181 (bottom left)

Copyright © George Tonikian
Page 126

Copyright © Sally Twigg
Page 158 (top)

Copyright © Sylvia van Heijenoort
Page 164

Copyright © Frank White Photography
Pages 30 (right), 40 (bottom)

Copyright © Woody Guthrie Center
Page 8

Copyright © Alexander Zayas / Kabik Photo Group
Pages 179 (top right), 181, (bottom right), 186 (bottom), 189 (top), 191 (center), 195 (bottom)

Copyright © Michael Zorn
Page 151

FROM THE TOM MORELLO COLLECTION
Pages 6, 13, 14, 15, 16 (top, left and center), 17, 18, 19, 20, 21, 22, 23, 24, 25, 26, 27, 29 (bottom right) 31, 32, 33, 36 (bottom), 37 (right), 41 (left) 42 (bottom), 47 (top) 53 (left), 59, 60 (top left), 61 (bottom), 63, 68 (top), 69 (bottom right), 71 (bottom right), 84 (top right), 100 (top right), 105, 125, 131 (top right and bottom), 132 (center and bottom), 142 (top right), 143 (right), 149 (right), 161 (bottom), 175 (bottom right), 182 (bottom left), 190 (center right), 194 (bottom), 198, 200 (unless listed elsewhere), 201 (unless listed elsewhere), 204
Photo by Antonella Alberti
Page 185 (second row, third from left)
Photo courtesy of Babygrande
Page 185 (third row, left)
Photo by Ryan Berena
Page 185 (bottom row, second from left)
Photo by James Chang
Page 185 (top right)
Photo by Marcus Haney
Page 185 (top row, second from left)
Artwork by Scott Hepburn / Dark Horse Comics
Page 201 (bottom row, second from left)
Photo by Maclay Heriot
Page 185 (top row, fourth from left)
Photo by Atiba Jefferson
Page 185 (third row, second from left)
Photo by Tak Kamihagi
Page 185 (second row, fourth from left)
Photo by Nikko LaMere
Page 185 (bottom row, third from left)
Photo by Joey Martinez
Page 185 (bottom left)
Photo by Dan Medhurst
Page 185 (second row, left)
Photos by Eitan Miskevich
Pages 179 (bottom), 181 (top), 182 (top), 185 (top left)
Photo by Niina Myller
Page 185 (bottom right)
Photo by Brit O'Brien
Page 185 (second row, right)
Photo by Zoe Rain
Page 185 (second row, second from left)
Photo by Rukes
Page 185 (top row, third from left)
Photo by Travis Shinn
Page 185 (third row, right)
Photo by Brain Ziff
Page 185 (third row, third from left, and bottom row, fourth from left)
Artwork by fans
Pages 202, 203

VIDEO STILLS
Copyright © Activision Publishing Inc.
Page 85

Copyright © New West Records
Pages 142 (bottom), 143 (bottom left)

Copyright © Nimbus School of Recording & Media
Page 41 (right)

Copyright © Sony Music
Pages 72, 73, 97, 102, 136 (left)

POSTERS
Copyright © Gerrit Serné (photography) / Cor Van Wees (design)
Page 54

INDEX

JUSTICIA VICTOR JARA
SOUTENIR LES GILETS JAUNES
NO TPP
FUCK TED CRUZ
CORNELL FOREVER
ΑΔΕΡΦΙΑ ΘΑ ΝΙΚΗΣΟΥΜΕ
BHINNEKA TUNGGAL IKA
21
ST. PAULI
END RACISM
BOURBON NOT BOMBS
FUCK KAVANAUGH
FUCK BREXIT